# “THE THREE [illegible] JUDGES”

*Rupert Eales-White*

# DEDICATION

*This book is dedicated to the memory of my beloved brother Gavin Cushny (né Eales-White). Gavin was a dual citizen of the USA and UK. He was murdered on 11th September 2001 by Osama Bin Laden. Gavin was working on the 104th floor of the North Tower, which the first Boeing Hit. Gavin was a man of enormous courage, indomitable will and hunger for life. Though trapped above the Boeing, he nearly broke free from the building. His body was found in a stairwell with another victim and twelve of those incredibly brave New York firemen. He did not die alone.*

# ENDORSEMENTS

*"An intriguing story that attracts interested reading, offering curiosity, subtlety and extraordinary humor in a tale about the everyday reality of judicial decision-taking".* Baron Ouseley

*"A challenging and disturbing read, highlighting though provoking issues regarding our judicial system".* Dr Howard Cohen, General Practitioner.

*"A compelling story told persuasively and with patience and humour".* Colin Soden, member of Mensa, retired Banking Executive and Company Director.

*"Rupert's self-deprecating humour brings a light touch to the tenacity displayed fighting the good fight against Positional Power, and, through this book, succeeding."* Bryan Smith, long time Editor of the journal – Industrial and Commercial Training.

*"A disturbing narrative, with some Kafkaesque moments, showing how easily the citizen can be dragged into a bureaucratic nightmare".* Martin Pexton, Personnel Director of Allen & Overy 1990-2002, Corporate Development Director of London Merchant Securities 2002-7, MD of LMS capital 2007-9.

# 1. The facts speak for themselves

On the 5th October 2008, I drove my daughter Sophie and her best friend Bridey to an away match in Kingston-upon-Thames. They played in the Surrey under 14s football league.

I drove my car, a Nissan X-Trail, onto junction 6 of the M25, came off at junction 9 and drove towards Kingston on the A243.

About a week later, I received an official notification from the police that I had been involved in an incident with another car and "fled the scene of my crime" – driven off without stopping.

This was a bombshell, shortly followed by a letter from an insurance company, advising me of the name of the other party and that he would be claiming against me. We will call the other party John Smith.

This is a copy of the letter I wrote to Alice Brown of the local criminal investigation unit, dated the 27th October 2008.

*Dear Alice*

***ALC Ref: 41/06/103579/K***

***I AM COMPLETELY GOBSMACKED***

On Sunday 5th October, I was travelling from Warlingham to Kingston with my 13-year-old daughter in the front and her best friend in the back. They both play in the under 14 Surrey girls football league.

I turned off the M25 at Junction 9 to take the A243. As I came around the roundabout, there was a deep indentation in the road, which I did not see. However, I swerved slightly, recovered and proceeded on my way. No other car was involved. My daughter did look behind and saw another car do the same thing.

As no other car was involved, I cannot for the life of me believe this is the incident, for which I have received your statutory notice.

I proceeded along the A243 and was approaching traffic lights. I noticed, on my left, that a car was just starting to reverse onto this very busy road. The car had not actually moved and was positioned in the middle of the driver's very limited parking space in front of his house. I use the word "him". I could not see what the driver's gender was.

I realised that, to allow her/him to get out would require an emergency stop on a very busy road. This would have caused an accident, as the car behind me was "right up my backside" and would have crashed into me. I proceeded to drive on, slow down and park behind the large van that had already stopped. The traffic lights had just turned red.

I dismissed the incident from my mind. I did remark to the girls: *"I pity the poor sod that has to reverse onto a very busy road whenever he wants to drive from his house. He must be permanently stressed out of his mind."*

A few moments later (and I made no connection between the two events at the time), I noticed, in my rear-view mirror, a man running towards my car, exhibiting extremely aggressive body language – gesticulating for me to stop. (The lights had turned green and I had just started to move away.) The man managed to reach the car and thumped on the back of it.

I accelerated (safely) away. When driving on my own, it is not my practice to stop, when a man runs aggressively towards my car.

When I am responsible for the safety of two 13-year-old teenage girls, it is a golden rule. They were quite shaken up, as they had not fully recovered from the first incident.

I have now received the enclosed copy letter from X Insurance company.

Assuming I am right that the man was John Smith, if it is not too much trouble, could you ask him to withdraw his claim immediately.

Could you also caution him to stop forthwith running aggressively towards cars in the future – especially when the car contains young teenagers, who become quite frightened, when a strange man runs aggressively towards them, and violently hits the car, in which they are travelling.

I have sent a copy of this letter to X insurance company.

Many thanks

Yours sincerely

Rupert Eales-White

*Notes*

The key contents of this letter subsequently formed a "Statement of Truth" that was signed by myself and the two girls. Bridey signed with the consent of and in front of both her parents

I was duly asked to present my insurance details to a local police station, which I did, and on the 30th January 2009 I received a letter from them saying that they were dropping the matter and left me open to take civil action against the claimant.

I did not involve my insurance company, as I knew that I was innocent, and did not want to put my no claims bonus at risk.

In early November, I received another letter from X insurance company, enclosing the repair bill, which had been paid by them. They claimed that my violent swerve had caused the claimant's collision with another car, presumably, as what the claimant's car hit was not specified. I was a 100% responsible.

If I did not pay the sum of £1420 within 14 days, they would take me to court. (I lost this letter or threw it away, as I had no idea of what was to come)

This was my reply, dated 10th November 2008:

Dear Claims Director

**Claim Number:** 156803044568
**Policy Number**: VRSCK1379000200
**Your Policyholder**: John Smith
**Incident Date**: 05/10/2008

I will quote from my letter to which you refer:

*"I turned off the M25 at Junction 9 to take the A243. As I came around the roundabout, there was a deep indentation in the road,* ***which I did not see.*** *However, I swerved* ***slightly****, recovered and proceeded on my way. No other car was involved. My daughter did look behind and saw* ***another car*** *do the same thing".*

Three points:

1. As I did not see the indentation, I went through it. I did not, as you wrongly suggest, swerve to avoid the indentation.
2. It was a slight swerve. As I have a four-wheel drive, I regained control very quickly. I did not impede any other car.
3. My daughter saw another car do the same thing. She has advised me that the swerve was much more pronounced – but had looked back before seeing any consequences of this much more violent swerve.

I am not responsible for any incident whatsoever. Either the more violent swerver was responsible or the ultimate responsibility rests with whatever authority left a deep indentation in the road.

I do not expect to hear from you again.

Yours sincerely

Rupert Eales-White

I realise now that I should have the word "mug" written not only all over my face, but covering my entire body, head to toe. There is an argument, quite a strong argument, (with which my beloved wife would undoubtedly agree) that the general rule is that I should not be allowed out of the house, and the occasional exception is only when I am on a very short leash.

Over a period that lasted just over a year and a half, I was endlessly providing information in the form of ammunition, instantly used against me.

I have no idea, of course, what tissue of lies Mr Smith told his insurance company, but they simply clutched at the straws that I had kindly provided.

In any case, I was very worried about this threat of legal action and phoned them up. I did not speak to the person on the letter, but some other guy, who referred to the data on the electronic file.

I explained that I was at a complete loss as to why I was being claimed against, as nothing had happened. He kindly said that I could ignore the threat of legal action and he would talk to the claimant to get further information and get back to me. Incidentally, I never received any further communication from them.

More importantly and interestingly, he revealed to me the fact that Mr Smith had been travelling with his wife, who had taken down the details of my car registration number and it was he who had tried to stop my vehicle

Now this case is a mess when it comes to locations. I did not take in precisely where the location was. I knew that there were only two possible locations. The first was at the roundabout at junction 9, which became referred to as the A24 location (the reasons will become clear later). The second was at the traffic lights about a mile and half up the A243 to Kingston.

I did retain the police final clearance notice which stated that the claimant had reported a *"collision at the A243, Leatherhead Bypass, Leatherhead"*. I subsequently referred to the second A243 Kingston location as the A243, Leatherhead.

What I did pick up on instantly was that the claimant seemed to be claiming a collision, which had not taken place, had taken place in two different locations!

================

After the police clearance on the 30th January and, given that X insurance company had gone completely quiet, I assumed that that was the end of the matter and dismissed it from my mind.

I received the following letter from LCS (**L**ying, **C**heating **S**olicitors), dated 26th February 2009.

Dear Sirs

**Our Client**: John Smith

**Incident date**: 5th October 2008

I have instructions from our client to pursue a claim for damages arising out of the above accident.

I understand that the accident occurred when our client was driving along the road and you turned across the path of our client's vehicle.

In those circumstances, I consider that you were at fault because THEY (!!!) failed to keep a proper lookout for other road users and drove across the path of our client's correctly proceeding vehicle, thereby causing a collision between the two vehicles.

(And so on)

The total had gone up slightly to just over £1,440 and they added the standard phrase. *"If I do not receive a cheque in settlement in the next 14 days I will proceed to issue legal proceedings against you."*

I have often wondered if THEY were a Freudian slip. The first line of the third paragraph refers to "you" and a few words later, it becomes the plural "THEY". (It was in normal case in the letter.) It is very unnatural in normal circumstances. The second "you" would be automatic – you would type it on automatic pilot, as it were.

I think it was a Freudian slip and it **was** Mr and Mrs Smith who had failed to keep a proper look-out for other road users.

I can never prove what happened, but my own view is that there are two credible explanations.

1. Mr Smith was, in fact, driving the vehicle that was far too close to my rear end for my comfort, which is why I did not stop to let the reverse parker proceed. Mr Smith had, for whatever reason, taken his "eye off the ball". He realised that he was about to hit my car from behind and, as he would be 100% liable for this collision, swerved instinctively to his left (not out into the oncoming traffic) and caused the damage by hitting an inanimate object.

That would have taken a few seconds to recover from, his wife to take down details of my car, and him to run after me and thump on my car in an act of aggression.

He was clearly an aggressive man and declared in his witness statement of the 8th April 2010 that he had "taken his medication for (high) blood pressure". People who are frequently aggressive tend to suffer high blood pressure.

Aggressive men also tend to instantly blame anyone but themselves, when things go badly. So, it was entirely feasible that he blamed me, as I had caused the accident by driving too slowly (as I slowed down to stop at the traffic lights) and, if he had been quarrelling with his wife, it would make a lot of sense to put the blame entirely on me to avoid a blame game between him and his wife.

What would have made matters much worse for me is that he would have convinced himself that he was telling the truth and I was telling lies. This is frequently the case with Jekyll and Hyde characters (see note after reason 2).

What would have made it even worse is if the police had reprimanded him for aggression, probably unlikely. At some stage however, he would have read my letter to the police.

So, Mr Smith hated me for telling the police that he was an aggressive, Hyde-driven (as it were) man, rejected the filthy lie and wanted to *"shoot the messenger"*

If this is the case, then it means that LCS were in cahoots with him from the very off.

2. It was a case of mistaken identity. It was not my vehicle in the first place.

*Note:*

Our subconscious brain (SB) is a much more powerful decision-taker than nearly all of us care to recognise.

Indeed, whenever we lose (conscious) control, whether we are asleep or have drunk too much alcohol or have thrown a temper tantrum or hissy fit, or we have been overcome by the red mists of rage, or we are acting in the heat of the moment, our actions are driven by our SB (Subconscious Brain). They are unintentional, and we cannot control ourselves. In the heat of the moment, we are unable to "get a grip".

No-one intentionally kills a stranger in an act of road rage, is sentenced to 10 years in jail and destroys their own lives and the lives of their nearest and dearest.

So, when we are in the grip of a temper tantrum, we are overcome by hideous, hidden Mr Hyde, with our actions driven by SB (**S**ubconscious **B**rain).

Those in Hyde mode, and we have all been at the receiving or giving end, become very aggressive and use "twisted" logic.

They:

- Adopt an arrogant, condescending tone of voice, treating you as a mentally retarded 3-year-old.
- Mount a sustained attack on your opposing point of view.
- Very unhelpfully introduce points you have not made as the key plank of your own argument. They then destroy these points with consummate ease. They, of course, only introduce

points that they can rebut with masses of evidence. You become angry at this totally untrue and unfair "twisting", playing straight into their hands, as the last thing they want is for you to remain calm and rational or "cool".

- Invariably introduce early on, as part of the cunning, subconscious distraction strategy, some fault you have, which is completely irrelevant, or some behavioural incident you have already apologized for (a couple of million times). This is to reduce your self-esteem from the dizzy heights of a mentally retarded 3-year-old to the depths of a slowly dying crushed slug.
- Only bring into play opinions, presented as facts that support their position.
- Crush any counter arguments by this twisted logic (driven by self-centred emotion and not the facts and so requiring the facts to be "twisted", sometimes out of all recognition,
metamorphosing into downright lies).
- If that fails, shout you down.
- If that fails, stomp off, claiming victory.

In any case, once I read this bombshell letter, I was not amused. Well, I was furious. I wrote the following angry letter back, dated 27th February 2009.

*Dear Ms Croaker*

*I am extremely annoyed at a further issue of a threatening notification to me. I would like them to cease forthwith.*

*Before we look in detail at the facts, I would refer you to the third paragraph of your letter. You consider me at fault because "they" (presumably Mr and Mrs Smith) failed to keep a proper look-out for other road users! I suggest Mr Smith issues legal proceedings against himself for failure to keep a proper look-out and therefore having an accident with another vehicle.*

*Let us turn to the facts:*

1. *I draw your attention to the letter I wrote to the Police after receiving their statutory notification.*
2. *In a subsequent conversation with X insurance company, it was established that it was the second location, where Mr Smith got involved in an accident with another car, which has never been identified.*
3. *So, Mr Smith ran aggressively ran towards my car, thumped on it and frightened two 13-year-old teenagers – a matter for civil action on my part for significant damages for violent, aggressive behaviour, do you not think?*
4. *The insurance company man, who issued the same threat as you have and the same claim for damages, agreed that they needed to revert to Mr Smith to establish evidence in the case, which has been singularly lacking to date.*
5. *The police have dropped the matter.*
6. *Both I and the two girls can bear witness to the fact that my car was not involved in any collision, nor did I do anything except drive on the inside lane in a straight line within the speed limit to the relevant traffic lights, at which time Mr Smith initiated his highly aggressive action towards me, my car and the two girls.*

*Yours faithfully*

*Rupert Eales-White*

This would, of course, not have done Mr Smith's blood pressure any good at all. His hidden Mr Hyde would have been thirsting for revenge. Any logical, rational thoughts would have long disappeared. I, without any conscious recognition of this fact at the time, was not very rational when I wrote that letter – driven by righteous anger.

Hindsight is a wonderful thing. I was plotting my own downfall – not a very sensible thing to do, really.

## *THE CLAIM*

On the 8th April 2009, LCS duly filed a claim against me in the appropriate county court.

The pertinent points made were, and I quote verbatim:

1. The accident occurred on the A24.
2. The accident occurred when the Claimant was driving along the road and the Defendant's (the word 'vehicle' was missed out) turned across the path of the Claimant's vehicle.
3. The accident was the Defendant's fault because they failed to keep a proper look-out for other road users and drove across the path of the Claimant's correctly proceeding vehicle, causing a collision between the two vehicles.

### Statement of Truth

The Claimant believes that the facts stated in these particulars of claim are true.

I am duly authorised by the Claimant to sign this statement.

Full name: Bertha Liar
Name of Solicitors firm: Lying, Cheating Solicitors
Position or office held – paralegal (junior dogsbody)

So, this A24 location became, in my mind, the first location, where the mild swerve took place without any contact with another vehicle. In all letters subsequently, I referred to this as the A24, following LCS's lead.

You will notice that there is no reference to a roundabout and there is no reference to my famous swerve.

It was not until 3 days before the final hearing on the 21st April 2010 when I printed off a Google map that I realised that I had never travelled anywhere near the A24. I know – Burk, Burk, Burk, Burk, and Burk!

However, I was confident that I had enough ammunition in my locker to ensure victory.

As you can imagine, I put in a very detailed defence indeed, running to 13 pages with all the attachments. Amongst many other things, I delivered what I thought was the coup de grace, in addition to the fact that I had consistently and persistently maintained that I had not been involved in any collision.

What I did was to point out that, if I cut across the claimants correctly proceeding vehicle along the road, then he would have hit my car on the left-hand side and only damage to the front or right-hand side of his vehicle could have occurred.

Given that the repair bill demonstrated **only** damage to his left-hand side (replacement of the left-hand wing being the main item), then his statement of truth was a tad on the untrue side.

Summarising my defence, I pointed out that the claimant had claimed that a non-existent collision had taken place in two different locations – the A243, Leatherhead to the Police and the A24 via LCS to the Court.

I sat back, licking my lips, genuinely looking forward to the hearing. I had been advised in the bumph, which I had got from the court, that the next step would be for us to be called to a hearing in front of a district judge in the Small Claims Court.

# 2.Irrational judges (IJs) intervene

Instead of advice as to the date of my eagerly anticipated hearing, on 14 May 2009, I received the following:

> ***GENERAL FORM OF JUDGEMENT OR ORDER***
>
> *Before* ***DISTRICT JUDGE IJ 1,*** *sitting at Y County Court (*and address*)*
>
> *Upon the Courts own motion. The Court has made this order of its own initiative without a hearing. If you object to this order, you must make an application to have it set aside, varied or stayed within 7 days of receiving it.*
>
> ***IT IS ORDERED THAT***
>
> *Defendant to file and serve a properly detailed defence pursuant to CPR 16.5 by the 29th May 2009 and if the defence be struck out and the Claimant be entitled to enter judgement forthwith."*

My reaction to this extraordinary notice was, *"What the F*** is going on? The claimant had claimed in less than half a page and my incredibly detailed defence had run, with attachments, to 13 pages precisely."*

The order is not written very clearly. I was not quite sure what the threat was – but clearly there was a threat there. In the light of subsequent events, I realise that the order should have read: *"The defence to file and serve a properly detailed defence pursuant to CPR16.5 by the 29th May. Failure to provide such a defence will result in I, the judge, striking out the existing defence and awarding the case to the claimant."*

So, I wrote back (next day delivery) pointing out that I had produced a very detailed defence, asking what more I needed to provide, and could they postpone the deadline so that I could produce an even more detailed defence (once I knew what more I had to put into it) than the one already submitted.

The sound of silence

Then I got the identical formal notice from **IJ2**. This was dated the 26th June, received in the post on the 30th June, and stated: *"The date for compliance with the order of 14th May be varied to 4pm on 29th June 2009!"*

My postage costs have been phenomenal in this case. Frantic "next day delivery" letter back asking for advice of what more I should provide over and above the very detailed defence I had already submitted and asking for postponement of a deadline that was impossible for me to meet.

I then wrote to the judge, who had issued the second notice, on the same day I received it - 30th June, (again next day delivery) with the following:

Dear District Judge

I would refer you to the 'facts of the matter' attached and would be grateful if you would use your powers to dismiss the claim.

I look forward to hearing from you soon.

Yours sincerely

Rupert Eales-White

**FACTS OF THE MATTER**

**Evidence already provided to the court**

- No collision took place. (I can, if necessary, provide a witnessed statement from both teenagers that no contact with another car, never mind a collision, took place throughout the entire journey)

- The claimant reported one location of the "collision" to the police, and a completely different location to the courts via his solicitors.
- The laws of Physics mean that it is impossible that I cut across the claimant's vehicle "correctly proceeding" along the road and caused damage **only** to the left-hand side of his vehicle.

**What should have happened?**

The case against me should have been dropped.

**What has happened?**

- A district judge used his powers to bypass the traditional resolution in the Small Claims Court and advised me on the 14th May that he took the power to resolve against me and I had until 29th May to comply with the courts pro-forma requirements, of which I am completely unaware.
- I replied by special delivery asking for postponement, confirmation that the evidence already provided was sufficient or, if not, what was the extra information I needed to provide.
- On 30th June (today), I received a notification from another district judge, dated the 26th June, advising me that they had moved the date forward for compliance to the previous day and gave a specific time, i.e. 4 p.m. There has been no advice as to whether I had already complied or what extra I needed to do to comply.
- I replied by special delivery the same day asking for a further variation, giving a month's gap between receipt of notification and the actual date, as well as repeating my unanswered request to know whether I had complied or what I should do to comply.

- I am understandably concerned that the judge may have already found against me, as I have necessarily failed to comply with the deadline.

Rupert Eales-White

It is amazing how stupid I am. I realised, as I was inserting this letter into the text, that, although I had put the second judge as "another" district judge, necessarily, as I had no other name in the frame apart from the first IJ, the letter was addressed to the same judge.!

I should have Googled the entire list and written to a different judge – but it simply did not cross my mind at the time. I had no idea, of course, that I was dealing with irrational judges driven by a specific UREB (see note) to ensure I was found guilty, irrelevant of the facts of the matter.

<u>*Note:*</u>

Deliberately going slightly ahead of the story line but giving the minimum information away, in January 2010, I contacted an individual, who had become a literary agent after retiring from a career as a barrister. I will call him by his initials – JAS. In a phone conversation in the same month, and I quote verbatim, JAS said to me:

***"I have witnessed and been part of numerous perversions of the course of justice by judges, driven by an unrecognised bias against the defendant."***

I call these unrecognised biases (and prejudices) UREBs – **U**n**R**Ecognised **B**iases

They are derived from what are called negative limiting implicit beliefs, as I found out when studying in 2001 for a diploma in coaching.

Beliefs can be explicit or patent – consciously held and driving our intentional behaviour. Beliefs can be implicit or latent – subconsciously held and driving our unintentional behaviour. This is why *"old habits die hard"*. According to the Neurological Programming Society (NLP), if we successfully repeat a new behaviour at least 20 times, it becomes a habit and the beliefs underpinning the new behaviour form in our SB to ensure that the now habitual behaviour carries on ad infinitum.

Where our behaviour is driven by implicit beliefs, it is impossible to change, as we are unaware of the existence of those beliefs

Now I have worked in/written about the people development since 1990. The number of occasions when an individual, ranging from junior employee to executive, has genuinely committed to a positive change in behaviour as a result of a feedback process is legion. The number of occasions when said individual has completely failed, despite the best of intentions, is also legion. This does very little for their feelings of self-esteem and confidence or improving their career prospects.

This situation arises where their behaviour, which they genuinely want to change, has been driven by what, as mentioned above, are called negative limiting implicit beliefs, e.g. a woman's place is in the home, as compared to positive enabling beliefs, e.g. there is good in everyone.

There are a considerable number of negative limiting beliefs driving bad behaviour and the most common are the ego UREB or *"I am the best thing since sliced bread, nay a divinity to be worshipped by all lesser mortals and all mortals are lesser than me"*, the racist UREB or implicit racism, the sexist UREB or implicit sexism and the homophobic UREB or implicit homophobia.

Indeed, there has been significant shift from explicitly held negative limiting beliefs to implicitly held negative beliefs and behaviour, driven by UREBs.

Let me explain. When I was born (27th January 1952), what I call iron societal laws prevailed as they were based on very strongly held beliefs that had been in place for centuries. The key beliefs prevailing as regards white men and women were that:

1. The man was intellectually superior to the woman. *"Don't worry your pretty little head about it my dear."*

2. The man was the *"hunter-gather"*, the *"sole bread-winner"*, the *"King of the family castle"*, who should *"rule with a rod of iron"*
3. The woman, a member of the *"fairer sex"* should raise a family, with the duty of producing a *"son and heir"*, *"honour and obey"* her husband, *"stand by her man"*, and carry out all the domestic duties – become a domestic slave, not goddess.

As regards black people, they were considered ignorant savages, who had smaller brains than white people, and who should focus on sporting activities where they had an unfair competitive advantage due to superior physiques to compensate for their mental weakness.

They were referred to as "coons", "darkies", and "gollywogs" with the most common epithet being "niggers". Hence the phrase "nigger in a wood-pile" (which means "fly in the ointment") and the rhyme: *"Catch a nigger by the toe. If he hollors, let him go."*

The only other non-white people living in the UK at the time were the Chinese. This is the doggerel my mother frequently repeated to me:

*Chinky, Chinky Chinaman feeley very ill.*
*"Chinky, Chinky, Chinaman takey biggey pill.*
*Wakey in the morning, feeley very well,*
*Pulley back the bedclothes, poofey, what a smell.*

As regards homosexuals, referred to as "queers", "poofs" or "faggots", they were perverts, who indulged in illegal, unspeakable, unnatural sexual practices.

These strongly held beliefs formed what is termed a conscious collective mindset which determined the societal norms of behaviour. If an individual deviated, then they became social outcasts or pariahs - joined a leper colony, as has become the fate of smokers today.

So, the clear majority of men and women held explicit racist, sexist and homophobic views. Today, we live in an age of enlightenment, where the right messages have resounded down the decades that we should value the richness of diversity and be treated equally irrelevant of our "colour, class or creed", gender and sexual orientation.

Repetition of messages can change our beliefs – as will be explained in the context of the story.

However, where beliefs are very strongly held, they simply move from above the surface (consciously held) to below the surface – in the hidden depths of our SB.

A final point, before we return to my story, is that the law is an ass, as it fails to take into account the difference between intentional and unintentional behaviour. The definition of Malice Aforethought is completely wrong, the result of which is that many individual citizens are convicted of murder, when it should have been manslaughter.

'Malice Aforethought' is defined as, '*The CONSCIOUS INTENT to cause death or grievous bodily harm to another person before the person commits the crime……but does not, necessarily, imply any ill will, spite or hatred towards the individual kille*d".

To prove malice aforethought is the key requirement to deliver a sentence of first degree murder.

However, afore is the archaic use of the preposition 'before'. So, there should be new legal terminology, Malice Afterthought, defined as "*conscious intent to cause death or grievous bodily harm to another person*" (There is no need for the rest of the sentence, as it constitutes pleonasm – the use of more words necessary to convey meaning, and the phrase after ……. is completely incorrect and belongs to the next definition.)

The correct definition of Malice Beforethought is, "*subconsciously-driven intent to cause death or grievous bodily harm to another person---but does not, necessarily, imply any ill will, spite or hatred towards the individual killed*". An example would be the man who kills a stranger in an act of road rage likewise.

There is only one set of circumstances I have come across, where the judiciary to a man (or a much less visible woman or the almost non-existent black person) apply the correct definition of Malice Beforethought, and never give a sentence of first degree murder, and often do not even, quite rightly, send the offender to prison.

This is the case where one of the partners or spouses is a controlling type (often, but not always a man), who frequently goes into excess and frequently verbally and physically abuses the other partner or spouse (often, but not always a woman), who is a caring type. It is referred to as the "Battered wife syndrome". She goes into excess care mode and turns into a worm or doormat.

She reaches "the end of her tether". One hit or insult is the "last straw" which breaks the camel's back. The worm turns. She snaps. Action and reaction are equal and opposite. She is instantly overcome by hideous Mrs. Hyde, who hates her oppressor with an unbearable intensity. Mrs. Hyde seizes, say a kitchen knife, and stabs her oppressor to death. Once the deed is done, Mrs. Hyde disappears completely.

She then "comes to" in a state of shock and disbelief. She espies the knife, which she has zero recollection of taking or using, and drops it to the ground. When talking to the police, she says words along the lines of: '*I don't know what came over me. It was as if I was a completely different person*'

================

Returning to my story, there was no reply to my letter – just the sound of silence

Then **IJ2** replied. I had come back from holiday in France on 5th August to receive the usual notification. I had to reply by the Friday, I think it was. I glanced at it, threw it away and gave up.

The formal notice I received was dated 12th August 2009

**JUDGEMENT FOR THE CLAIMANT**
**(In default)**

**To the Defendant**

You have not replied to the claim form.

It is therefore ordered that you must pay the claimant £1529.41 for debt (and interest to date of judgement) and £177.00 for costs

You must pay the claimant a total of **£1,706.41** forthwith

**Warning**

**If you ignore this order your goods may be removed or sold, or other enforcement proceedings may be taken against you. If this happens, further costs will be added.**

Author's note:

I will also quote from the relevant notes for the defendant.

**Notes for the defendant**

If you did not reply to the claim from and believe judgement has been entered wrongly in default, you may apply to the court office giving your reasons why the judgement should be set aside.

Details of this judgement will be entered in a public register, the register of Judgements, Orders and Fines. They will then be passed to credit reference agencies, who will supply them to credit grantors and others seeking information on your financial standing.

**This will make it difficult for you to get credit.**

**If you pay in full within one month,** you can ask the court to cancel the entry on the register.

Once I had read this, I reached a low point. Ever since I got the first extra-ordinary order from IJ1, my mind had been in turmoil. Why were these judges behaving so irrationally – flying in the face of clear irrefutable evidence?

So, I immediately wrote to the Court Office, enclosed my detailed defence and used, as my grounds of appeal, the fact that I had indeed replied to the claim form.

This was the reply on 25th August 2009.

*Dear Sir/Madam*

*Re: Mr Smith v Mr Rupert Eales-White*

*Case No: 7RSP07770*

*Thank you for your letter of 23 August 2009. Although you did submit a defence the Judge ordered it to be struck out. As judgement has already been entered, you will need to apply to have is set aside on form M135. You will then receive a hearing date. There is a fee of £75 payable when this application is made, unless you qualify for fees exemption.*

*Yours faithfully*

*Miss A. Bird*

Note:

Well I did qualify for fees exemption, as I had lost all my business a few years earlier and had not been able to make any money since. My net loss as a sole trader for the current fiscal year was over £7000 and the capital I had taken from the business I had put into liquidation was nearly exhausted. I had cashed in my personal pension plan early, which yielded £11,000 a year.

However, I had no intention whatsoever of seeking qualification for financial assistance, but the sum I had been ordered to pay was a very significant amount in the overall scheme of things.

So, I filled in the form, with the key documents that proved "beyond a shadow of a doubt" that the claimant had claimed a non-existent collision had taken place at two different locations, but also asking the judge (who would preside over my hearing) to ensure that none of the judges who had acted so irrationally presided, as well as asking for an explanation for their irrational actions. The three questions I asked were:

1. *Why I had no reply to three requests for what additional information I needed to provide over and above the detailed defence submitted and filed?*
2. *Why, as soon as I failed to comply with the thrice changed deadline for a reply, which I could not make, my defence was instantly "struck out" and the adverse judgement made against me?*
3. *Why, as the normal process once claims are submitted is resolution in the Small Claims Court, the expectations set for me, a judge decided to override the process?*

Matters got delayed. My entire documentation was returned, as I had failed to make the cheque out to the right body. It had not been specified in the documentation I received when I was "judged against" and I had lost the documentation accompanying the original bumph, when I had to pay various fees for the privilege of entering a defence against the claim.

So, I sent them all back with the right payee.

Time was marching on. On 8th September, I received a letter from LCS, the relevant section being:

> *"If I do not receive payment, I will take immediate steps to enforce the judgement without telling you in advance (for instance by sending Bailiffs or High Court Enforcement Officers to your house.) You will then have to pay any additional costs our client incurs in enforcing this judgement against you."*

Well this did not do a lot for our collective peace of mind, especially my daughter Sophie, just turned 14, who started to hide her beloved lap-top under her bed, whenever she went to school.

I wrote back to both LCS to call off their hounds and the Court to call off LCS's hounds on the basis that the case was under appeal (which LCS knew very well, of course). No bailiffs turned up and after a few weeks, my daughter left her lap-top out in the open again.

Then, when I was running on automatic pilot on a training run for the New Forest Marathon, my subconscious brain very kindly indeed (ta very much, SB) solved the problem for me.

So, I provided the solution to the Judge and asked for a **black judge** to be appointed to preside over my case!!

# 3.Why? Oh! Why?

Now I have deliberately omitted a key fact. In early May 2009, both the claimant and the defendant were sent something called an "Allocation Questionnaire" to complete. You were allowed to call on an expert witness in your defence (or to support your claim). So, I called myself as an expert witness in the psychology of human relationships.

I then provided a written explanation as to why, in my expert opinion, the claimant had acted so aggressively towards me and why he had claimed that a collision with my vehicle, which had not actually taken place, had taken place in two different locations. (Yes. I am a stupid, arrogant so-and-so. However, that is not, traditionally, a sufficient nor necessary condition for an innocent man to be found guilty)

I have not got the document but I can recall, as already mentioned, that I explained that Mr Smith was a Jekyll and Hyde character, did not recognise his aggressive nature, that his ego UREB had acted to "shoot the messenger" and, also, that he wanted to avoid a "blame game" with his wife, who was the passenger on the left side, where all the damage had occurred [!], and so the claimant was driven to externalise blame on to me.

Note:

Remember that any documents submitted to the court had also to be sent to the claimant's solicitors!

At the time, I could not provide third party evidence for my expertise. This was subsequently provided by Jonathan Bond, the Director of HR and Learning at Pinsent Masons (a top City law firm), who wrote the foreword to *"Succeed at Work – take the fast track to the top"* (published in October 2009 by Management Books 2000 Ltd), in which one of his comments was: *"Rupert displays an extra-ordinary number of psychological insights."*

Now the first draft of the book had been completed and Jonathan was reading it, before composing his foreword, at the same time as I received the allocation questionnaire.

So, to prove my expertise, I sent the judge, who was to preside over my hearing the following section of chapter 1." Achieve All Your Goals", which demonstrates how any individual can achieve any goal they set themselves.

## "WHY BARACK OBAMA WON THE ELECTION

My thesis is that Barack Obama only won the election because 80% of those, who were subconsciously racially prejudiced against him and would have cast their votes against him, changed their minds due to personal self-interest (PSI).

To prove this thesis, we look at the:

- Formation of subconscious racial prejudice.
- Demonstration with the "Bradley effect".
- The poll position before the economic crisis.
- The consequence on voting outcomes.
- Why Barack was Mr Cool.
- Why the economic crisis played to Barack Obama's strengths.
- The impact on votes cast in the election.

### *FORMATION OF SUBCONCSCIOUS RACIAL PREJUDICE*

We can develop biases and prejudices, which operate from our subconscious, and are not consciously recognised as that would cause an unacceptable loss of self-image and self-esteem. I have called such entities UREBs, which stands for **URE**cognised **B**iases (and prejudices)

They come into being as our parents bombard us with a series of messages, frequently repeated over a prolonged period of time.

A given message impacts on our subconscious and progressively seeps into our consciousness without us being consciously aware. I call this process SPO which is short for **S**ubconscious **P**sychological **O**smosis. With enough repetitions, our conscious behaviour changes as a result. As we do not know the source, we assume that we have consciously made the decision or altered our behaviour. We cannot therefore consciously control the behaviour, which leads to "inner tension".

Some parents are consciously racially prejudiced, and the consistency of words and actions mean that their children follow suit.

Some are subconsciously racially prejudiced. That prejudice produces racist behaviour that is repeated over time. Due to the power of SPO, the children become subconsciously racially prejudiced. Whenever there is a gap between words and deeds, it is the deeds that have most impact – hence *"actions speak louder than words"* and *"Don't do as I do. Do as I say."*

Individuals, who have a subconscious racial prejudice cannot, of course, change the conscious demonstration of that prejudice, driven by their racist UREB or, simply, implicit racism.

You can pick up this prejudice using distancing language, e.g. "them", "those people", accompanied by a negative tone of voice and body language.

In my opinion, Margaret Thatcher never saw black people as "one of us" and was subconsciously racially prejudiced against them. Due to the power of SPO, that subconscious prejudice was transferred to her children. This explains why her daughter Carol used, when she was no longer in front of the cameras and thought that she was "safe", the somewhat distancing language of "gollywog". Naturally, she vehemently protested that she was not racially prejudiced as that was the conscious truth.

If you were to suggest to a subconsciously racially prejudiced person that they might be racist, they necessarily say: *"Me a racist, don't be daft. I have a friend who is black"*, rather than: *"I treat this friend as an honorary white. This enables to me to continue to be prejudiced, which I have to, as I do not know that I am"*.

The reality of both the existence of subconscious racial prejudice and the lack of conscious recognition is demonstrated with what is termed the "Bradley effect".

### *DEMONSTRATION WITH THE "BRADLEY EFFECT"*

Los Angeles Mayor Tom Bradley was the black Democratic candidate to become Governor of California in 1982. His opponent was a white, Republican candidate. The closing polls **and** exit polls showed Bradley with a convincing lead of more than 10%. Tom Bradley lost narrowly.

What happened was that this 10% were subconsciously racially prejudiced. However, they had been consciously convinced that Bradley was the superior candidate on the arguments presented, consciously recognised. When they were asked the question by pollsters as to which candidate they would vote for, they told the conscious truth, which was all they could tell.

However, they were subconsciously racially prejudiced. They did not recognise this consciously, as it would be too great a blow to their self-image and self-esteem as liberal minded Democrats.

When they made the decision in the polling booth, the deed was done by their racist UREBs. UREBs always take over when you are faced with a vital decision that consciously you consider is the best one to take but is the opposite of what the UREB desires. UREBs appear and disappear in the twinkling of an eye.

The key point is that, at the conscious level, they did not know they had done the opposite of what they intended to do. Dr Jekyll did not know that his Mr Hyde existed nor committed heinous crimes in his name. So, when the 10% told the exit pollsters that they had voted for Tom Bradley, as far as they were concerned, they told the truth.

### *POSITION BEFORE THE CRISIS*

Before the meltdown of the banking system, the credit crunch and the perception (and reality) in the eyes of the American voter of a unique economic crisis, John McCain was neck and neck in the polls with Senator Obama – due to the "Palin bounce".

Sarah Palin was a "conviction" politician. She never put forward a rational argument in favour of a given position, supported by real facts. One reason is that she did not have any facts at her fingertips. Indeed, she resisted all attempts by her mentors to educate her into the facts before her three debates with Joe Biden. She was a very clever woman. She knew she had no chance at all in a rational discussion with anyone.

She also knew that arguments passionately put forward with utter conviction and using irrational logic ("facts" created, twisted or suppressed to support her position) would often win the day – George Bush and Tony Blair are recent examples as regards the Iraq War.

John McCain was also driven by convictions. However, he is a statesman – a man of enormous integrity and honesty – but hot-headed and prone to temper tantrums.

### *CONSEQUENCES ON VOTING INTENTIONS*

If the economic crisis had not erupted, then Barack Obama would have lost, even if well ahead in the polls, because the 10% who were subconsciously racially prejudiced against him, but consciously supported him, would have voted against him and, necessarily, lied to the pollsters in the exit polls.

The Bradley effect would have been confirmed.

There would have been much wailing and gnashing of teeth. The US would have been riven with discord and disharmony. There may well have been numerous riots by black people who had been robbed of the right result.

### *WHY BARACK OBAMA WAS MR COOL*

When Barack Obama was interviewed by the media on endless occasions over a two-year period, he came across as *"cool, calm, and collected"*. Adverse comments frequently made were that he was too cool, calm and collected – did not show enough passion and conviction. He was also *"cool, calm and collected"* during his 1-on-1 debates with first Hilary Clinton and then John McCain.

Two years of repeated messages, picked up at the subconscious level only, that Barack Obama was cool, calm and collected but lacked passion and conviction meant the voter had a very firmly embedded subconscious mindset that this was true.

## *WHY THE ECONOMIC CRISIS PLAYED TO BARACK OBAMA'S STRENGTHS*

A generally held view is that, if facing a crisis, you need a leader that is "cool in a crisis", has a "cool head". Quite right too. You don't need passion and conviction. They can lead to horrendous decisions. George Bush is a conviction politician, had a personal vendetta to revenge his father's humiliation by Saddam Hussein – hey presto! – the invasion of Iraq.

The collective subconscious mindset of the voter was that Barack Obama would be "cool in a crisis".

As soon as Lehmans crashed and economic meltdown threatened, Barack Obama obtained a significant jump in the polls – from level-pegging to a 6% lead, he maintained right up to the election.

Moreover, the economic crisis was by far the most important factor that determined which way the voter cast his secret ballot, as proved by exit polls.

## *THE IMPACT ON THE VOTES CAST IN THE ELECTION*

80% of the subconsciously racially prejudiced stayed true to their conscious intent. I reach this conclusion by the fact that, as mentioned above, the average poll lead in the closing polls was 6%. The actual result was a lead of 4%. This means that only 20% of the 10% subconsciously racially prejudiced voters remained true to their implicit racial prejudice. 80% voted as they had consciously intended.

The reason that the 80%, in the act of voting, overrode their UREB 's command is that they felt that they were or would become personally affected as the economic crisis unwound. They needed to vote for the man, they had a "gut feel" as "good in a crisis" – Mr Cool.

Personal self-interest typically lodges in the subconscious. Few people go around telling everyone including themselves, *"I am a selfish bastard"*. When there is a subconscious battle between personal self-interest and prejudice, personal self-interest always wins.

(Another example of how subconscious personal self-interest beats a subconscious negative driver, is that irrational emotional controlling types only stop beating their children, when these children grow large enough to hit them back and do serious damage. Such people do not consciously believe that they are "child abusers" and "cowards")

The reason that the 20%, in the act of voting, obeyed the racist UREB's sudden instruction is that they did not see themselves (with the thinking process a subconscious one) personally affected or likely to be sufficiently personally affected by the unwinding economic crisis to alter the balance of power between the two subconscious drivers, i.e. subconscious prejudice ruled OK."

================

Once I realised why the judges had behaved so irrationally, I sent another letter to the putative presiding Judge, repeating and then answering the three questions in my original letter.
Quoting from that letter:

***THE QUESTIONS***

1. *Why I had no reply to three requests for what additional information I needed to provide over and above the detailed defence submitted and filed?*
2. *Why, as soon as I failed to comply with the thrice changed deadline for a reply, which I could not make, my defence was instantly "struck out" and the adverse judgement made against me?*
3. *Why, as the normal process once claims are submitted is resolution in the Small Claims Court, the expectations set for me, a judge decided to override the process?*

***THE ANSWERS***

*Once, I had sent the section of the chapter, you have just read, entitled "Why Barack Obama won the election", I sealed my fate.*

*The two judges, who read this section, very briefly indeed consciously recognised that they themselves, due to their own parenting, had been brought up to be subconsciously racially prejudiced and therefore had made poor judgements in the past due to the actions of their racist UREBS, of which they had not been consciously aware and to which they could not, therefore, consciously admit.*

*As the hitherto "hidden truth" was completely unacceptable due to the impact on self-image and self-esteem (which would be at a very high level due to their august position in the community) and the natural desire to seen as high-performing competent judges that they think themselves to be, it was viciously and emotionally kicked back to the subconscious to become a "still small voice" or "prick of conscience".*

*They became irrational, emotional controllers with subsequent actions taken by their UREBs.*

*The messenger, i.e. my good self became a "dirty little liar" and was instantly, (deservedly in their eyes) and thoroughly "shot". Then I was shot again and again, til I was a twitching corpse – pay £1706.41 (from my gross pension of 11,000 a year as I had no advances and have not yet received any royalties), threatened with the bailiffs and so on.*

*So the answers to my three questions are:*

1. *I had already submitted a watertight defence. So, there was no more information that I could provide. When a judge is acting like Sarah Palin or George Bush, i.e. driven by their UREBs, then facts are completely irrelevant and very, very inconvenient.*
2. *"Vengeance is mine", Sayeth the Judge – an interesting interpretation of the English judicial system.*
3. *"Vengeance is MINE", Sayeth the Judge. It was essential to the revenge mission that no other party was exposed to the rational defence case, as that might cause, "some awkward questions". It was vital that I was not present."*

This letter to a Judge was sent via the lowly lady in the Court Office, who has been the only individual to write a polite letter to me and sign it. Her real name (as I have changed all the names to protect the guilty) was Mrs G. Friend, and a true friend she turned out to be. Thank God, she was female.

I asked her to use her discretion as to which Judge she approached with the letter.

She did, bless her, and the judge at my hearing exactly one year to the day (5th October 2009) after the actual event was Judge Right – the "Fair, female Judge" of the next chapter.

I tried to keep emotions under control at all times. One has too. But it has been tough. Having re-read my letter to focus on the key extracts, I shall finish this chapter with my final comments in the letter to the judge - and I am not, normally, a religious man.

> *I had to act very swiftly indeed to ask for a further postponement and for what additional information I needed to provide over and above the very, very, very, detailed defence submitted and filed.*
>
> *Answer came there none.*
>
> *For the third time, "The cock crew". Then I was lead to the cross and crucified.*
>
> ***Please remove the nails that are still sticking in my hands and feet"***
>
> *Rupert Eales-White*

# 4.The fair female Judge – Judge Right

I went to Court exactly one year to the day after the incident had taken place, i.e. on 5th October 2009. It was one of the most stressful events of my life. I had never been before a judge until now. I was 57 years old at the time. I had no idea what to expect – but I managed to stay cool on the outside most of the time.

It was a nightmare before the actual start. It was scheduled to start at 2.p.m and everyone but everyone had gone to lunch. There were only two people around – a woman who was checking the contents of the bags and brief cases and a man who was, when necessary as the result of a bleep, doing a body check after you had been through the metal scanner.

Once through, I identified on the "notice board" that my case was to be held at 2 pm and heard by Judge Right (name changed, of course), though her gender was not specified.

However, there was one set of courts in the building and a completely different set in another building and I did not know where my case was being heard.

Eventually, I plucked up my courage to ask the man, when he had a lull, where I should go. So, I went up some stairs and into a room where there was a seething mass of humanity. You had to report in and be ticked off, before you were summoned to see the judge.

The catch twenty-two was that the time that the office re-opened after lunch was the same time as when your case was heard – 2 p.m. An additional stress was that there was a long queue to resister your presence. I kept my cool at the conscious level, but I was a nervous wreck inside.

Most, if not all, had a legal representative, who would have put them straight. Nevertheless, it is about time that the courts moved away from the middle ages and moved into the 20th century, as a helpful transition to the 21st.

The start should be to treat people as if they are human beings and simply (if they cannot introduce the concept of lunch-time cover) have an information desk.

Also, given my experience of lawyers and the fact that this was a minor matter, there should be changes so that individuals can represent themselves, if they so choose, without the dice being so incredibly weighted against them.

Before we were called, a very snotty nosed individual identified herself as the claimant's lawyer (the claimant was nowhere to be seen), did not introduce herself and we proceeded to the court room, where I discovered, with a heartfelt sigh of relief, that the judge was female. (Clearly there was no black judge available)

*Note*

I called this lawyer SS - The **S**limy **S**olicitor (or German patriot seeking after truth). She was also at the final hearing on 21$^{st}$ April 2010.

The proceedings were quite short, full of legal jargon, which went completely above my head and, at the end, Judge Right's ruling was that the judgement against me was to be set aside and the matter settled in the Small Claims Court, where it had been originally destined, before the IJs had intervened with their racist UREB inside them.

I am not black by the way. My father claimed he could trace our ancestry back to 1208 and a certain Robert White. At the beginning of the 18$^{th}$ century, a Dr Eales (who had no children) left all his money to a close friend Major White, on the condition that the first-born male was called Eales-White, subsequently extended to all children by my great grandmother, who was a terrible snob.

The point is that they had a personal UREB against me, along the lines of, *"I hate Rupert's guts as he is a dirty, filthy, little liar. He has dared to suggest that I am racially prejudiced, which everyone knows is a complete and utter lie, as I am whiter than white!"*

Judge Right was very helpful, though I did not appreciate just how helpful she had tried to be until 6 months later.

First of all, apart from the vital and just decision of setting aside the irrational ruling of the IJs, she suggested that I hired a lawyer or went to a Citizens Advice Bureau and obtained legal aid. My wife strongly supported her. They were both right and they were both wrong.

They were right in that, with a lawyer on my side, I think that LCS would have retired gracefully from the case and I would have saved about £1,800.

They were both wrong. If I had done, then I would not have suffered the utter travesty of justice that ensued, which would have diminished the quality and richness of this book. I hope to get the fine back with the royalties from the book.

In any case, I was busy writing the series books, knew that obtaining legal aid would be a very time-consuming, and was not desperately impressed by my experience of lawyers to date. More importantly, I carried with me the Sword of Truth and, very naively, I thought that that would see me through.

One other significant way she helped me was to ask a question on my behalf. She asked SS who would be present at the hearing. SS's reply was that it would be the claimant's wife and not the claimant!

Judge Right also suggested that I presented a purely factual "Statement of Truth" - no more rousing of racist UREBs.

Finally, she also helped me very much with her judgement, dated the 26th November 2009. I had already put in my "Statement of Truth" on 18th October (copied to LCS including a signed witness statement by myself and the two girls), as I had been advised that you had to put all new material in no later than 14 days before the court hearing or it would be disallowed.

There was a postal strike threatened. I had a hernia operation scheduled on 3rd November, and I was terrified that I would receive a notice in the post advising me to attend a hearing that had already taken place!

The hearing was set for the 21st April 2010, and the claimant had to pay into court £100 by the 14th December (a date which they could easily miss as they were very slow off the starting blocks) or the case was awarded in my favour, and they was the following delightful direction:

> *"In deciding the case, the court will find it very helpful to have a sketch plan and photographs of the place where the accident happened"*

I chuckled at this, given the problems presented by Judge Right to LCS in drawing up a sketch plan of a non-collision in two different locations. Silly, deluded fool. In hindsight, I should have made a special trip back to the location, at which time I would have developed knowledge of the topography and realised that I had never been near the A24 and only on the roundabout at the end of the Leatherhead bypass.

The problem was that I was fully confident that they would drop out – could not face the Sword of Truth. Also, Judge Right's directions were full of comments that the court should be advised, if we had settled matters before the hearing, which is why she had put it so far into the future.

Judge Right had assumed that LCS would act rationally.

It is only in the act of writing this section at 1.00 am on Monday the 26th April, that I realised that I had aroused very large UREBs in the lawyers. There is a repeated theme coming through this narrative. I should be locked up for my own protection.

When I sent a copy of my Statement of Truth to LCS, I had sent it to the paralegal who had signed the witness statement, as she was the only name I could identify. The solicitor SS at the hearing did not introduce herself. The letter threatening to send in the bailiffs had no name at all – just an initial.

I asked her to pass it on, but also pointed out that she had signed a false "Statement of Truth", might be guilty of contempt of court and should seek advice from the Citizens Advice Bureau.

When I did eventually get a copy of Mr Smith's witness statement on 7th April 2010, I got the same treatment - an initial and no name. However, the reference at the top started with three initials.

I must say, I did take inordinate pleasure when I replied with my letter starting, "Dear ARS"!

As to why Judge Right was so helpful, I would imagine that she would have been a very annoyed lady:

1. Seeing the male UREBs in action in the courts on a regular basis.
2. In career terms, suffering the glass ceiling effect due to the male-dominant judicial establishment being dominated by explicit or implicit sexism.
3. The regular inappropriate behaviour towards a female judge from a number of her male colleagues, dictated by their UREB *"a woman's place is in the home"*, but consciously denied as existing. (One of the most horrendous realities of frequent UREB attacks is that the "truth of the matter" is inevitably denied and frequently thrown back in your face as being your behaviour and not theirs – a classic case of projection.)
4. Recognising, as the result of regular UREB attacks that she had personally experienced, that my sword was a Sword of Truth and that there were rampart racist, sexist and homophobic UREBs around in a lot of her male colleagues.

<u>Notes</u>

Now early bits of a book called *"The Hidden Truth – ensure our citizens are never convicted of crimes they did not commit"*, have been in a very draft form since September 2009, when I realised why my defence had been struck out.

In early January 2010, I wrote to Judge Right (having found out her Christian name from Google) providing her with a copy of a draft of the first chapter and asking if she might like to write the foreword, on an anonymous basis, and just send it unsigned in the post.

The reply from the Office Manager (I was upgraded from my friend, the lowly office clerk) was quite revealing.

"Dear Mr Eales-White

I refer to your letter dated 9th January 2010 which was addressed to District Judge Right.

District Judge Right has asked that I respond to you on her behalf and return the papers which you sent to her. She further requests that I explain that she is sorry that she is unable to enter correspondence with you.

Yours sincerely

Miss L Black, Office Manager."

# 5. The calm before the storm

Everything went very quiet and stayed quiet.
Then, I received in the post on 7th April 2010, the following letter from ARS.

Dear Mr Eales-White

**Our Client**: Mr J Smith

**Incident Date**: 5th October 2008

We write further to the Notice of Hearing in this matter and in order to comply with the District Judge's Directions.

Please find enclosed, by way of disclosure, the Claimant's (WHAT?). Please confirm whether these can be agreed.

We confirm that the Claimant intends to rely on their own oral. Written statements are enclosed.

(Followed by a squiggle and LCS)

I was very worried that the claimant was going to rely on his own oral – sounded very unpleasant. As to what I was going to find, by way of disclosure, I half expected some of the claimant's dried spermatozoa in the envelope. I would have preferred his, "head on a platter".

Now Judge Right's written ruling was that no statements were permitted within 14 days of the hearing and those, correctly submitted, should be copied to the "other side". Though the letter was dated 1st April, I got it on the 7th April, when the bar was in place.

So, either their material would be judged inadmissible or they had already submitted it, and this was a smoke-screen. In any case, if a judge gives you written instructions, I try to follow them. So, this put me under enormous pressure.

I opened it at 3p.m. I was very keen to copy my reply to the Court manager to pass on to the presiding judge. As the local post office was closed, I had a 5-mile journey in the knowledge that next day delivery had to be completed by 5 p.m.

My witness statement had been posted to LCS on 18th October 2009 – again giving them as much ammunition they wanted to create what was an entire fiction.

The statement was 5 pages long. The original statement a year earlier had been less than a third of a page. What a phenomenal memory Mr Smith had – such an eye for detail, recalling events that had taken place over 18 months earlier, as if they had been only yesterday.

If I had had a couple of weeks to think, carry out research, especially when it comes to location, it is just conceivable I would have the won the case.

No, I am being a bit of an optimist, as always. I could have proved that I was standing on the moon, when the collision took place, and I would have still been ruled against – see next chapter, **"The Stitch-Up".**

## THE CLAIMANTS WITNESS STATEMENT

I divide this up into:

- Painting a picture
- The collision
- The chase
- My response

### *PAINTING A PICTURE*

Paras 1 to 7 were devoted to painting a picture of a man,

- Who was the safest and most careful driver on the planet.
- Who was calm and cool and cried when a petal died, slightly marred by the phrase, *"I had taken my daily medication for blood pressure."*
- Whose relationship with his wife was such that it made Romeo and Juliet look like a one-night stand.

## *THE COLLISION*

**Para 8**

I had driven north along the A24 road and had then driven onto the A243. I was driving towards a large roundabout when I intended to take the road for Oxshott and Esher. I was positioned in the right-hand lane of a dual carriageway and I was travelling at about 50 mph. At this point in time I was just passing under what I would call an underpass under another road. I was driving a steady course in my lane.

**Para 9**

Quite suddenly I was aware of a black or dark 4X4 vehicle type vehicle that was passing me in the left-hand lane, undertaking me in fact. As it passed, it cut across to its right very close to me and I felt a **bump** as it did so. I immediately swerved to my right but because of the location I was in, there was a wall to my right along the centre island at this point. I virtually immediately swerved back again to my left.

**Para 10**

I realised that the 4X4 had **struck** me. (The rest of this para fits into the next section)

### *Key Points*

We will look at why there was an initial use of the word "bump", followed by "struck" with the word "crash" (used in Para 7) in the next chapter, **The Stitch Up",** when IJ3 carried out his masterclass.

Now we look at the map of the location.

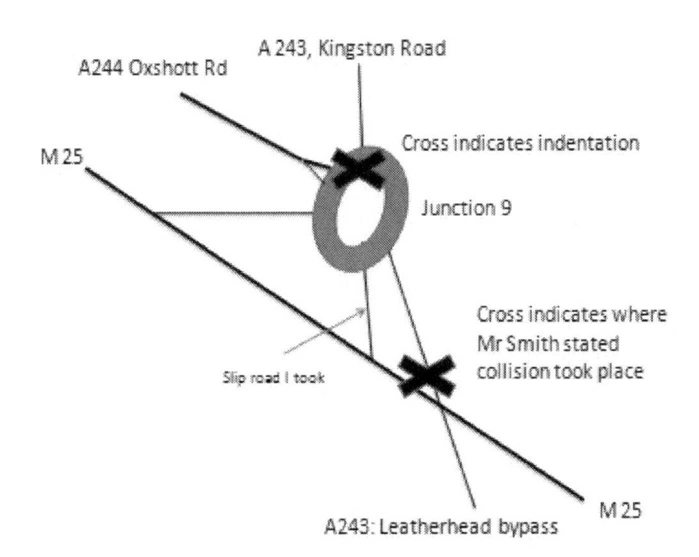


### *Key Points*

The claimant and LCS had been (had it not been for their guardian angel IJ3, who presided at the final hearing) hoist by my accidental misinformation petard.

As you know, as reported to the police on the 27th October 2008, I had advised them that I had come off the M25 at junction 9, gone around the roundabout and proceeded onto the A243. As I had already told them in the opening paragraph that I was travelling to Kingston upon Thames, the fact that it was the A243 to Kingston, not Leatherhead, was taken as read and so implicit.

The work "Kingston" was never used and, as mentioned earlier, I had followed their lead, and, on all subsequent, quite numerous occasions, I had referred to the location as A243, Leatherhead.

They had been subject to SPO or **S**ubconscious **P**sychological **O**smosis.

So, the claimant knew and LCS knew "for a fact" that I had been travelling on the Leatherhead Bypass, Leatherhead, and so could create the compelling scenario of reckless Rupert "bumping", "striking", "crashing into" this poor innocent man, travelling steadily and safely about his business.

Now I had made the assumption (Oh! woefully inadequate amoeba that I am) that, if I provided to the judge at the hearing clear evidence that I had not been where the claimant had claimed that I had "bumped" into his car ("struck" or "crashed" into his car) and I had never been anywhere near the A24 location, that would do the trick nicely.

Silly me. As said before, I could have proved that I had been having a leisurely stroll on the dark side of Mars at the time of the "collision" and I still would have been found guilty as charged.

The point is that I paid no attention to the underpass and did not realise that he was passing under me, when I was travelling above him on the M25, until I wrote up the hearing – see next chapter, **"The Stitch-Up"**

*Note:*

I have just realised this in the act of writing. Freudian slips are worth noting and analysing. When you tell a "tall story", it is very unwise to make it pure fiction. You want to collide with the actual truth as much as you can.

Now what I have hypothesised (and I am increasingly beginning to believe that I am right) was that he was quarrelling with his wife, the love of his life (who was going to represent the inseparable duo without the claimant present, according to what slimeball told Judge Right and, in fact, was nowhere to be seen on the day), swerved sharply to the left when he realised he was going to hit my car and, it is quite clear now, crashed into a wall on the left. (Incidentally, as mentioned, his entire left-hand wing had had to be replaced. It is amazing what havoc a little bumph will do)

So now, he kept the “the wall” but switched directions, and, of course, could not actually hit the wall and so had to put all the damage down to my “bumpcrash”. I wonder if there is a wall on the right-hand side of the Leatherhead Bypass – probably not.

## THE CHASE

**Para 10**

I realised that the 4X4 had struck me. I followed and flashed my lights at the vehicle, but he continued to drive towards the roundabout. I **requested** my wife to write down the registration number of the 4X4. She noted it as VT55PQ3, which was however, slightly incorrect (*see Key Points*). I followed the **black** 4X4. It negotiated the round-about and then took the Chessington exit towards Malden Rushett *(This is the A243, Kingston*). I decided I would follow until a suitable opportunity to stop and speak to the driver presented itself.

**Para 11**

We arrived at a set of traffic lights which were red. I stopped behind the 4X4 and I got out and walked towards the driver’s side of the vehicle to speak with the driver. I am not an aggressive sort of person and all I wanted to do was to speak to the driver about the incident. I tapped on the driver’s window. The male driver looked towards me and I can only describe his reaction as looking totally startled as if he was not aware that I was there.

**Para 12**

At that moment the lights had changed to green and the 4X4 had accelerated away. The driver did not attempt to open his window and to speak with me. I did not see any passengers in the 4X4. I cannot be totally sure, but it may have been fitted with darkened privacy glass. From the moment that the 4X4 struck me until the vehicle drove away from me at the traffic lights, I did not lose sight of the vehicle.

***Key points***

Mr Smith is a factor worker, with, I would imagine, a rather large racist UREB inside him, (if not explicitly racist), which would mean that he would have another reason to loathe me intensely.

As well as claiming to be the safest driver on the planet, he must be the most erudite factory worker in the world, and have an eidetic memory, given his total recall of the incident that took place over 18 months earlier.

Your subconscious will have noticed the frequent repetition of the title of the next chapter, **"The Stitch Up".** This means that you will have consciously concluded that I was stitched up, before you have read the chapter that proves that I was stitched up.

The very frequent use of 4X4 was deliberate, as was the phrase "darkened privacy glass" (all my glass is clear, though now it contains but tasteless dregs) to suggest that I was a wealthy, stuck-up, inconsiderate, environmentally unfriendly individual. I am as poor as a church mouse and bought a 4X4, when I was earning some decent money, for two reasons:

1. I wear glasses and find the glare of night-time traffic very off-putting. In a 4X4, with much greater height, I can now proceed at the normal speed because the lights on dip show much more of the road ahead.
2. I live in a remote setting with a single-track road and some hills. When the snow falls, it is never cleared and during the very snowy conditions, if I had not had a 4X4, my wife would have been unable to go to work for a whole week. She teaches a reception class. The road was only manageable by 4X4s. Indeed, my neighbour had to abandon his car as did 3 strangers. All four cars were torched by "travellers" living about a mile and a half away in a caravan site. My neighbour's replacement vehicle was a 4X4.

All the references on the letters, all the names and my registration number gave been changed. His wife had got everything right except the last digit/letter. She saw, or so it is stated, 3 and it is an R.

Notice that, originally, it was "black or dark" and then it became "black" only.

Notice also the Freudian slip. He **"requested**" his wife. Surely not, sir. Surely, you meant: *"I turned around to the love of my life and said, 'my darling, my poppet, my little angel, sweetheart and soul-mate', would you mind awfully taking the number of the car, which has just caused me to crash into a wall, whilst I run after him with my knuckle duster and beat the living hell out of him'"*

I wonder whether Juliette did not turn up in court because she was black **and** blue.

Finally, it is worth noting that, according to his written statement, he said that: *"The male driver looked towards me........totally startled"*. The reason will become clear in the next chapter, **"The Stitch Up".**

<u>*Note*</u>

I will cover this point off now, as I never had a chance when I had my day in court, as UJ3 (I have decided to rename the first 2 judges UJ1 and UJ2 and the third UJ3, with U short-form for UREB driven) took the unusual stance of an impartial "seeker after truth" of treating everything the claimant said in his witness statement as the Gospel according to UREBs (and by implication everything I had said as lies) – see next chapter. You may recall the title, but just in case you don't, the title is, "**THE STITCH-UP".**

I was going to make the telling point that the probability of me telling porkies was incredibly low. Not only did it mean that the two girls were also telling porkies, not only did it mean that we have a reverse memory process (the further from the event the better your memory) but it also meant that I had, completely voluntarily, put myself at risk of a prison sentence.

You may remember that I had asked the police to have a word with Mr Smith about his aggressive behaviour. If they had done (and they might have done), then, if he was innocent, his protestations would have convinced the police, who could have charged me with "trying to pervert the course of justice" and "wasting police time".

I am sure that the former charge, if I had been convicted of the offence, would have a possible jail sentence to go along with the criminal record.

## MY RESPONSE

Well, I was at panic stations. I did a very rush job and wrote the following letter to ARS, wrote a covering note to Miss Black, the Court Manager, pointing out I was necessarily one day late with my reply and provided her with a copy for the judge, who was to preside. Clearly the letter was dated and posted special delivery on the same day as receipt – 7$^{th}$ April 2010.

> Dear ARS
>
> **Your client**: Mr J. Smith
> **Incident Date**: 5$^{th}$ October 2008
>
> It would be most helpful if, when signing letters, you gave me a name to reply to, rather than a squiggle or the initials in a reference. I would also point out that I only received the letter today, 7$^{th}$ April. Unless you have submitted the statement without my "agreement", then you are inside the 14-day period.
>
> We will deal purely in facts or witnessed statements. First of all, you ask whether your Claimant's written statement can be "agreed". I assume you mean whether I consider that it is a fair reflection of the "truth of the matter". As I don't, I cannot "agree".
>
> In terms of attempting to get to as an impartial picture of the truth from a purely factual basis, I would firstly refer you to the "Statement of Truth" signed by me and the two passengers where we stated that, at no time, during the

entire journey, did my vehicle come into contact come with another vehicle.

Now you reported to the court that the claimant's vehicle and mine were involved in a collision at the A24 location – the roundabout when I came off junction 9 of the motorway. In para 9 of your witness statement, there is reference to a "bump", which caused over £1,400 of damage.

There was not even a bump. I draw your attention to my reply to the Claims Director of Toyota Insurance, dated 10th November 2008. These are the facts of the matter. Incidentally, I notice that in para 8, the phrase is "**I felt a bump**". In para 10, it becomes, "**the 4X4" had struck me.**"

Now there are the somewhat bizarre paragraphs 11 and 12. I draw your attention to the letter I wrote to Alice Brown of the Criminal Justice unit. This was when the incident was very fresh indeed in my mind. The last two paragraphs of the first page set out the facts of the matter.

There is a phrase that, "memory plays tricks on us". I wonder whether that phrase applies to your client.

Yours sincerely and cc Miss Black

I then had a flash of inspiration on and realised that, if both Statements of Truth were actually true, then the one right logical answer was that it was a case of mistaken identity. I was not the car involved.

So I sent, next day delivery, a letter to ARS pointing out that conclusion and suggesting that he or she should consult with her client with a view to withdrawal from the case, copying the letter in to the Court Manager.

Finally, I got around to studying the location on Google Maps, discovered that I had been at neither of the locations claimed, but, as it was only 3 days before the hearing, I just printed off 4 copies and took it with my bulging brief case. I had 6 sets of stapled papers.

You may ask why I had not spent much more time on what was a vital court case, discovered the underpass and so on. The trouble was that I was working under horrendous pressure to meet a deadline for the final draft of one of the series books, as well as continuing my domestic duties and support role to Sophie and my wife.

I had been under continuous pressure since before the case started. I had been commissioned to write the series by Management 2000 Ltd in January 2009. By the time of the final court case, the following had been published.

"Succeed at Work" and "Succeed in Life" October 2009

"Succeed as a Leader" and "Succeed as a Parent" January 2010

"Succeed with your Team" and "Succeed with your Partner" April 2010

The deadline for "Succeed as a Runner" was the 30th April, with publication taking place in September.

The tragedy was that we had just entered the deepest recession since the Great Crash of 1929 and it turned out that Management 2000 had no muscle in the market-place. There was no marketing and none of the series books were available in any of the retail outlets. At the time of the Court case, I had received the princely sum of £108.41

# 6. The Stitch-up

Have you ever been stitched up? I am sure you have. We all have and sometimes we do the stitching up ourselves. I was well and truly stitched up towards the end of my first career in banking. We will call the case study, "TWO UWs" [ U stands for UREB driven and the W stands, obviously, for Bankers]

**TWO UWs**

I have this rather fanciful notion that I am reasonably intelligent. It does not matter how intelligent you are, you can be stitched up and are almost, (not quite), a spectator as you watch the skilful seamstress finishing off the final stitches in the body bag that contains your corpse and, more in sorrow than in anger, as you have realised the inevitable is, in fact, inevitable, observe, quite dispassionately, as the body bag, containing your lifeless entity, is thrown over the cliff top into the dark depths of the seething sea, never to be seen again.

About 9 months before I was first stitched up, in April 1987, I had been appointed the bank's first group strategic planning manager, reporting to a section head – UW1, who, in turn, reported to the head of central planning department.

The head honcho was a truly inspirational leader, we got on extremely well, and he had orchestrated my promotion from a more junior role in the same department.

UW1 was a very dry individual and a fellow of the Chartered Accountants – need I say more?

Now his boss, my sponsor, did not care about status and used the right man for the right job. So, totally unintentionally, I pissed my boss off, partly because he lacked imagination and creativity and was in charge of some-one who had quite a lot – so that made him look small (and alerted his ego UREB) and also because I took on a number of roles that were, "above my station", and "put his nose out of joint".

So, his ego UREB went on full alert, but bided its time. The head of department was replaced by a cultural conformist, i.e. a status-oriented control freak, who had hardly any imagination – a soul-mate for my boss. He was UW2.

It did not take long. A few weeks after my sponsor had left, I was summoned into the new head of department's office with my boss. They both advised me that it was in my best career interests, having only been in post for 9 months of my 2-year tenure and being a group high-flier, that I took a sideways move into the awesome job of manager of job evaluation systems! (UREBs are very, very spiteful creatures, as well very cunning. They must have spent some time determining the job I would hate most in the world.)

I fought the good fight. I was utterly powerless. What I had was two irrational Mr Spocks, if you can have such a thing. They weren't Mr Hydes, as they were "calm, cool, and collected" – no temper tantrums or rants or raves. They were irrational in that, like Mr Hyde, they twisted everything, ignored any "inconvenient truths", made things up and created new truths, which would normally be called "lies".

It was all done in the "best possible taste" and this so-called intelligent individual was led like a lamb to the slaughter.

Before we move on to make the connection to the matter in hand, the outcome was rather amusing. I accepted my lot and went off to be interviewed by my new boss. It was supposed to be a shoe-in.

Unfortunately, I asked my new boss a series of penetrating questions, which proved that the job was a waste of time and I was the last person on earth to be considered for it.

On 21st April 2010, over twenty-two years later, I was stitched up again. This time it was by UJ3, the judge presiding (playing the role of the head of department), with the able support of SS, playing the role of my former boss.

Now I turned up in plenty of time and anxiously scanned the "notice board", advising which judges were judging which claims. There were four judges in action, and my heart sank to my boots, not only when I saw that there was no Judge Right, but also when I saw the name of UJ2. However, although I read that my case was to be heard at 10 a.m., they had not, as previously, put a name against the frame.

All was, perhaps, not lost, as you could not identify gender. However, my hopes were not very high. I was pretty sure that it would be a male judge, as there as so few women judges – given the prevalence of the sexist UREB.

I did notice that one of the four judges presiding was only a deputy district judge.  I got the deputy, and he shot me. I would imagine that UJ2, riddled by his UREB and a visceral hatred of me, had taken this deputy to one side and said, *"If you want to earn your spurs and get to full district judge, then rid me of this turbulent priest"*. However, I am an optimist, which I am beginning to think is a terrible mistake, and I still had my Sword of Truth to wage against the forces of evil.

So, I registered, espied SS talking to an individual, whom I assumed was the claimant, as well as a young man. I don't know who the young man was, but the claimant was obviously the claimant, being much, much older. (Remember that Judge Right had been told by SS that his wife would attend and not him!  They must have spent hours and hours grooming this naturally aggressive old man.)

I sat in a seat, when I could get one, close to the party. (It was like British rail, overcrowded, with lots of people forced to stand, and lots of "passengers" sitting, having placed a bag or brief-case on the chairs next to them to stop anyone sitting down beside them).

I did this deliberately and occasionally looked at the claimant to see if he would recognise me. He didn't. The case was called, and I followed behind the party of three into UJ3's presence. I have no idea who the young man was. I would imagine that he was there to learn how to sew up a body bag.

Now UJ3 pretended that he had not had time to read all the papers (although he could not help referring very dismissively to my psychologically based papers, which he had obviously read and, no doubt, I had briefly roused his racist UREB, who was thirsting for him to "shoot the messenger"), emphasised that he was in a rush and then proceeded to take an hour and a half (3 times as long as the previous hearing) to ensure that all parties came to the "one right answer" – the twitching corpse syndrome.

I think that I could have been much better at wielding the Sword of Truth and I soon realised that, in this court, like in the head of department's office, the one number that 2 plus 2 did not made was 4 - but I kept the body bag unzipped for over an hour and a half, which was no mean feat.

In any case, even if I had operated at 100% (rather than around 30%), it was, as they say, "a foregone conclusion", and all I would have done is delayed matters for a few more minutes.

To start with, UJ3, very kindly and graciously, set out the process, which consisted of the following:

> **SS makes her statement without interruption from me**. The judge of course can interrupt and clarify and, in this case, consolidate the case for the claimant.
>
> **SS then puts the claimant on the "witness stand"** to embellish the "unvarnished truth" with the admiration and confirmation of UJ3 (sorry, I should have said with the penetrating and unbiased questioning of the judge to establish the, *"whole truth and nothing but the truth"*)
>
> **I ask the claimant questions.** I only asked one, much to the two bullies' surprise and relief.
>
> **I take the stand** and set out my side of the story with UJ3 trying to pour holes in it and twist everything that can be twisted (sorry, I should have said with the penetrating and unbiased questioning of the judge to establish, *"the whole truth and nothing but the truth"*.)

**SS then questions me** using only closed questions (including many leading questions) to bully and browbeat – unsuccessfully, but the logic was irresistible and greatly admired by UJ3. If he had been allowed to, he would have applauded very loudly and very frequently.

**UJ3 summarises** - sews up the body bag. His condescending tone of voice and body language indicated that he was on a rational emotional high, if I can put it that way. He followed his acolyte's lead by using the identical chain of logic (based, of course, by both on the explicit assumption that everything J. Smith had said was true and the implicit assumption that I and the two teenagers had lied) and the same terminology, e.g. "on the balance of probabilities" (which became total certainty) or "stretching the chain of co-incidence too far" – not that those were the actual words used. I cannot recall the more prosaic terminology deployed.

**UJ3 passes judgement.** The coffin is nailed down and tossed into the grave or the body bag, containing my corpse, is sewn up, hoisted and thrown into the sea of lies.

**Celebration.** The two UREBs dance around my grave, hugging and embracing, toasting a job well done and waxing lyrical on how I was such easy meat.

Developing key areas:

## *SS RISES TO THE OCCASION*

Very early on, it was established that the claimant's lengthy "statement of truth" was dated 8th April 2010. This should not have been allowed according to Judge Right's written rules. But then Right is wrong, when you are going to ensure, "wrong is right".

Then, SS produced a map of the locations of the "collision" but could not introduce it as evidence without my permission. I gave my permission, but on the proviso that the four Google maps I had produced, specifying the location, were also introduced.

Their map was a hand-written scribble with no copies – another brilliant UREB driven manoeuvre – dropping a bomb shell to blow me up. As you will appreciate, any sudden change, perceived negatively, throws you completely off-balance and causes, for introverts, an instant drop in confidence and self-esteem, exactly what the UREB doctor ordered.

What was an early sign of things to come and the inevitability of the outcome was UJ3's very dismissive comment, when he glanced at my map: *"Oh! One of those Google maps"* with the appropriate condescending tone of voice. He made no comment, of course, on the scribbled mess, naturally, as he was holding the Turin shroud.

### *THE CLAIMANT CONFIRMS THAT HE IS A NOT TOO DISTANT RELATIVE OF GOD*

That was the whole object of the exercise. It was brilliantly done. A long lengthy process, ably assisted by UJ3, to establish that the claimant was a wise sage from whose lips pearls of wisdom and divine truths endlessly emanated.

### *I QUESTIONED THE CLAIMANT*

I asked the claimant just one question. It was: "Do you recognise me?" He hummed and hawed, and then I blew it. I must admit that, although I kept "cool, calm and collected" throughout, I was under a very heavy psychological burden – knowing by now that I had a biased judge Hydell-bent on convicting me - and dealing with a host of papers.

I pointed out that I had looked at him several times in the "ante-chamber" and he had failed to recognise me. He then confirmed from my lead that he did not recognise me and added that he had only seen the side of my face. Quoting his witness statement: **"THE MALE DRIVER LOOKED TOWARDS ME....TOTALLY STARTLED"**

<u>*Note:*</u>

- Now I am not a trained lawyer, skilled in the arts of bullying and brow beating using only closed questions, including numerous loaded and leading questions, always with the appropriate body language and tone of voice to indicate that the "hostile witness" or defendant has the IQ of a retarded chimpanzee.

- UJ3, of course, expected me to behave in that fashion, and it was with a tone of incredulity that he could not help himself ask me, *"Is that the only question that you are going to ask?"*
- I had not properly planned my strategy. I had very little time available for me to prepare and was far too over reliant on the assumption that all I had to do was to wield my Sword of Truth. I should have followed one line only – either the claimant was telling a load of porkies or it was a case of mistaken identity.
- The fact that he did not recognise me was consistent with the latter strategy. In any case, I had quite a multiplicity of papers to refer to and was already bleeding inside from the inevitability of the outcome – the dull ache of despair settling on my subconscious soul.
- The frequency and deepness of the stabbing by both parties meant that my life-blood was slowly seeping out, leaving pools of crimson red on the carpet.
- I did not even point out the inconsistencies in his statement, as I had nailed him in a lie. Clearly, he had not studied his script sufficiently well, but was fast on his feet. UREBs are very fast indeed on their subconscious feet.

### *SWORD SHATTERED*

Now I had been sitting a seat away from SS in a very comfortable situation. I had, as said before, six stapled sets of papers, which I was trying to juggle, but plenty of room. It was suggested that I took the stand, replacing the now defied claimant. When I got there, it was very pokey – a bit like a very undersized pulpit. There was no room for my papers. They could not be laid side by side, but on top of each other, which referred to six different sets of papers very difficult. This was an excellent UREB driven manoeuvre by UJ3, of course.

However, I raised my sword and delivered the truth. I repeated verbatim the claimant's original statement, untainted by my streams of helpful data to the opposition – the claim against me, dated 8th April 2009. I got my pre-rehearsed hand-movements in, indicating with my left hand the claimant's "correctly proceeding vehicle" and with my right hand my car "cutting across the claimant's correctly proceeding vehicle".

I actually pointed out that, according to the laws of Physics, it was impossible, under the scenario set out by the claimant, for there to be any damage to the left-hand side of the vehicle and yet that was where all and only the damage had occurred to the claimant's vehicle.

I have reached the conclusion that I suffer from Rupert's Reversal of Reality Syndrome. I have a dream, I anticipate an outcome, I make a plan and the opposite prevails. How did UJ3, the lead lawyer for the prosecution, deal with this damning and trenchant point I had made?

He dealt with it with a, "nod, nod, wink, wink." Talking to me as if I was a complete ignoramus, he pointed out that claims lodged by lawyers in "Statements of Truth" (and claims, generally, made by insurance companies for that matter) were very sketchy and often inaccurate (as anyone in their right mind knew) and it was only when you could talk to the witnesses that the truth of the matter was revealed.

Jesus Christ! The original statement was a very precise clear "Statement of Truth" that had been witnessed as being the truth.

This comment by UJ3 destroys one of the pillars underpinning our justice system. We know that UREB driven policemen, driven to get results will put pressure (often successfully) on a suspect to confess to a crime that he or she did not commit – particularly black people, because of the rampart racist UREBs that make the police "institutionally racist".

Nevertheless, rightly, signed "witness statements" or suspects "statements" or any "statements of truth" that are signed must be taken very seriously indeed by those who signed them. I am not a lawyer, but I believe it is a criminal offence to sign a "statement of truth" which proves to be a tissue of lies.

UREBs, as you know, make people turn a blind eye to the truth. The judge's UREB had made a complete travesty of the truth. However, I still I had a fair bit of fight left in me. So, I referred the judge to the map and pointed out that I had never travelled on the A24, nor on the Leatherhead Bypass. I was swatted like a fly.

The judge had mentioned earlier on that he was not very familiar with the location, though he had travelled on it once or twice before. He now, having studied the scribbled mess of a map provided by SS, became an absolute expert.

He told me that I had travelled along some underpass, which the claimant had travelled along and asked me, quite tetchily, to point out the location of the swerve, having asked me to collect the mess from him.

The map was drawn up so that the roundabout was joined by the A24 (it joins a completely different roundabout at the bottom of the Leatherhead Bypass) and the turning to the A244 Oxshott was put in on a completely separate round-about, which it isn't. It was therefore impossible for me to put my cross to indicate that I was crossing over in a straight line onto the A243, Kingston.

I had to pause quite a while, looking at this blot on the landscape, and UJ3 got very impatient with me. Reflecting back on it, this is why the sketch was so important and, of course, I had had no time to look at the sketch, as there were no copies. This is why I should have rejected its introduction and why the rule applies that you cannot introduce evidence not seen by the defence. There has to be "prior disclosure". This is why there is the 14-day rule.

In any case, my witness statement was a faithful recording of my original letter to the police and I had also pointed out that X insurance company had claimed that I had not been in a collision with the claimant's vehicle but had caused a collision by my swerve.

The judge had covered that awkward truth with his sweeping statement that Insurance companies make up things as they go along and, additionally and inevitably, all the numerous inconvenient truths were brushed under the carpet and never acknowledged.

Absolutely incredible. There used to be a programme called "Jim'll fix it". A biased judge can fix anything.

<u>*Note:*</u>

When I referred the judge to the original letter to Alice Brown, it must have worried him a little as he, voluntarily, stated; "*I am glad you have referred to this key document*". What his UREB was saying was, *"Shit, I could be in trouble here!"*

***THE SS DOESN'T QUESTION ME!***

There is no chance of "promoting discovery" of the truth of any matter, if only closed questions are deployed and twisted through deliberate use of leading or loaded questions. You only get discovery of the truth, if you use the open questions – what, why and how. Where, when and who are fact finding questions.

You must be very careful with "Why" when it is subjective, e.g. "Why did you do that", as compared to objective, e.g. "Why do cheetahs run so fast?", as subjective "Why", especially when accompanied by a harsh tone of voice and aggressive body language, is, and is taken as, criticism and invariably gets an aggressive (controller) or passive (carer) response.

Always use a warm tone of voice and open body language and it is helpful to have a preamble, e.g. "I would really appreciate the reasons why you chose this course of action".

Indeed, one of the research findings on outstanding negotiators is that they signalled a change in behaviour in advance. e.g. "May I ask you a question, please? So, "May I ask you a question, please?" "Of, course." "I would really appreciate the reasons why you chose this course of action."

Incidentally, this sort of questioning approach lulls UREBs into a false sense of security and often they reveal themselves without the owner realising. When you have asked what is termed a "perceptive probing question", then make sure you simply pause and wait patiently until the reply comes.

The owner becomes increasingly uncomfortable with the prolonged silence and the UREB rushes in to break the awkward silence. "Well, actually, I did have a bit of a row with the client". "Sorry to hear that, and do you mind letting me know exactly what caused this row?

Prolonged silence and then the UREB reveals more evidence of his existence, which can be used to prove he exists at a later stage.

Closed questions deny the truth ever emerging:

- *"Were you standing next to the murder victim, whom we have established you hated, with your hands covered in his blood"? "Well, actually..." "Just answer the question put to you – yes or no."* "Yes" – **30 years for murder in the first degree**.
- *"Well, actually, I was going to say that when I came around to have it out with him, I found him with his throat cut. Now I did not like him very much as he had been horrid to me. But I get upset if a little bird dies, never mind a fellow human being. So, I tried to stem the flow of blood. Before he died, he looked at me and asked for forgiveness. Of course, I forgave him. He died with a smile on his face."* One more, "**miscarriage of justice**".

As mentioned, SS adopted quite a bullying approach, spending a lot of the time glancing at UJ3, at whom I never looked. No doubt, he nodded approval and secretly applauded her every skilful move, as well as taking notes to reproduce, with great embellishment and at great length, in his summary to follow. Her irresistible argument was:

1. We had established that the claimant and I had travelled the same route along this underpass. (was so confused that I did not realise that the underpass was under the M25, I was travelling on, until I wrote to the Office Manager after the guilty verdict)
2. We had established that I had swerved and hit the car without my knowing it, (or so I had stated). UREBs always "cast aspersions". Previously, UJ3 had airily dismissed the extensive repairs as quite consistent with "bumping" into a car.
3. We had established that the claimant's wife had taken down my number plate, with minor error, but it was almost impossible for it not to be my car.
4. We had established that Mr Smith had followed my car and, when possible, that he had tried to stop me. It was "stretching the chain of coincidence too far" for that not to be true.

*Note:*

- SS was clearly a little worried that the claimant had admitted that he had not recognised me (my one minor triumph) – a weak link given his detailed witness statement. If he remembered everything else with such crystal clarity, he would surely remember the driver, who had looked startled directly into his face.
- She aggressively made the point that it was extremely unusual, if not impossible, for my car to be approached, unless it had been by the claimant.
- I replied that there were quite a few occasions, when people approached my car when stationary, e.g. some-one wanting to clean the windows or find out directions for a given location.
- What was unusual and had never happened before was a stranger running aggressively towards my car and thumping on the back of it – a small crumb of comfort floating on a sea of desolation.

## Case closed.

*Note:*

- What I found quite amusing, another small crumb of comfort, is that she used numerous leading questions to lead me to the one right answer for a given question, whether the one right answer was a "yes" or a "no".
- Invariably, I gave the opposite answer to the one to which I was being led by the nose to give. This did unsettle SS a bit. She always looked despairingly at UJ3, and, no doubt, got his full sympathy vote for my obduracy and ridiculous resistance to the inevitable conclusion to the proceedings.

### *SDJ3 CONFIRMS THE ONE RIGHT ANSWER*

I knew by now that the case was indeed closed. It was a lengthy summation. UJ3 was thoroughly enjoying himself. As mentioned, he followed and embellished the identical line that SS had taken, never referring, of course, to any of the inconvenient truths and regularly casting a little bit of doubt on my statement that I had not noticed the "collision".

He was probably subconsciously driven by the truth that a little bump could not have caused the extensive damage. It had to be a collision.

SS, when writing up the claimant's "Statement of Truth" had picked up on this, again subconsciously, and so had started with a "crash", felt forced because of my statement to introduce the "bump" and then finish with: *"I noticed that the car had struck me."*

(*"I see that you have been bumping into your wife quite a few times last night"*, is not quite as credible a line, when the police have taken a man into custody, after his wife has staggered into the police station earlier, with severe bruising, and the odd broken rib to go with her two black eyes, than the opening gambit, *"I see that you repeatedly struck your wife last night"*).

Also, there was a little bit of subconscious wrestling with the witness statement signed by 3 individuals that at no time had my car come into contact (never mind "bump") with another vehicle

UJ3 was extra-ordinary kind to me and explained how it was just about possible because of the height of my X-Trail and the distraction of controlling the "violent" (ignoring, of course, my witnessed statement of "slight") swerve that I had not noticed colliding with a car on my right.

Quoting the claimant's witness statement: *"Quite suddenly I was aware of a black or dark 4X4 vehicle type vehicle that was passing me in the left-hand lane, undertaking me in fact. As it passed, it cut across to its right.......and struck me".*

It is inconceivable that I would not have noticed this collision. (Much more importantly, when I told Soph about the verdict, she railed at me for not calling her as a witness and pointed out that not only were we travelling at around 30 miles an hour, when we had crossed over, but also that **THERE WAS NO TRAFFIC ON THE RIGHT-HAND SIDE**)

**It is standard UREB driven behaviour**. If a given UREB has suffered the death threat of being revealed as existing deep inside you, that UREB has not only to ensure that the messenger is shot, not only that the owner is proved "whiter than white", but that the messenger is proved to be the "dirty little liar" that he is.

## THE VERDICT

## "You have been found guilty of travelling in excess of 50 miles an hour, as you swerved going through an indentation, hitting the claimant's car on the right-hand side (without noticing either the car or the collision)"

Absolutely incredible. I would never have believed that this was possible. That this sort of thing is going on a regular basis makes me livid.

Note:

Incidentally, before I decided, for very good reasons, to go with the publisher of the series books to publish "The Hidden Truth", I had lined up an agent, who was a retired barrister - JAS, whom I have already mentioned. As he had read *"Succeed in Life",* he was familiar with the "psychobabble".

(UREBs drive their owners to use the word, "psychobabble", to belittle the truth, "psychological insights", and so reduce the probability that they are uncovered and brought to the conscious light of day - and death.)

As you know, he said that he had witnessed and been part of numerous perversions of the course of justice by judges (and we are talking about the full works – jury trials) as the result of a UREB driven bias against the defendant.

He had also witnessed the reverse - defendants, who were clearly guilty, getting off scot free. This is because they were "one of us" in the judge's eyes, or, more accurately, shared the same set of UREBs, who fell deeply in love with each other, (just like SS and UJ3)

Incidentally, the great philosopher and psychologist Carl Jung wrote in 1933: *"A typology is designed, first and foremost, as an aid to a psychological critique of knowledge......The valuable thing here is the critical attempt to prevent oneself from taking one's own prejudices as the criterion for normality*"

Our UREBs, clearly, are our prejudices. If we have the same set of prejudices as another, we see ourselves, psychologically speaking, reflected in their eyes – the only two "normal" people in the room.

It was a masterpiece of magic and deception. First of all, SS provided the judge with a "map" that maximised his options – put all three locations close together and made sure that the indentation was half way round a roundabout that did not exist – excellent confusion tactics.

Introducing it unexpectedly into court was a masterstroke – as any sudden negative change disorientates us and reduces confidence and self-esteem.

Then, the judge moves away from the original A24 location – as inherently unsafe. SS retains the "cutting across" bit of the original statement, changes directions to accord with the repair bill, and puts it into a safer location (or so it was assumed) and adds that I was travelling at more than 50 miles an hour on the inside lane, creating the impression of a reckless driver (the opposite of the truth and what, no doubt, was the truth for the claimant), having established that the claimant was the safest driver on the planet.

My reckless driving, with no consideration for other road users, was clearly a fact, given that I am a selfish, arrogant, environmentally unfriendly driver of a 4x4 with darkened privacy glass!

Then the judge is affected by SPO, the repeated reference to swerves and indentations not only in the case material but also on the day, and so has to focus on that "fact", (i.e. come to rest on the "swerve" location), when delivering his verdict.

### *GRACEFUL IN VICTORY*

As soon as the verdict was delivered, SS got out her calculator and UJ3 suffered a "prick of conscience". This is always the case, when a UREB has achieved totally victory.

So, SS claimed 8% in unpaid interest from the date of the invoice. The little prick persuaded her to accept 3% from 30 days after issue of the invoice. I am truly grateful to that little prick! I am not so happy that I was completely stitched up by the prick's racist UREB.

As regards LCS, they took hardly any risks at all. They knew that my historic papers would alienate any male judge, and that the probability of Judge Right hearing the same case was very low indeed and may, of course, not have been permitted at all, as judge Right had heard my appeal to set aside the original, "one right answer".

They also knew, no doubt from years of experience, that I had set myself up as a fall guy, as I had no legal representation.

With a judge acting on their behalf and them applying all the tricks of the trade, e.g. giving me a very detailed witness statement of total lies out of time, slipping in a single crude, grossly inaccurate diagram at the last possible moment, on the day, and so on, they were very confident that would it be a "stroll in the park", as indeed it transpired.

Funnily enough, I overheard SS tell the claimant that he had nothing to worry about, as they chatted amicably before the off.

*Note:*

When I was doing my first edit of "The Hidden Truth" on 14th May, I decided to Google LCS to discover the identity of ARS. I duly entered LCS into the bar, pressed and before looking at the contact list in their homepage, I was distracted by another heading for LCS, "**THE SOLICITORS FROM HELL**".

I looked inside and read the following about LCS. "*They have a tendency to spin a web of lies to get helpless innocent people convicted or slandered. If you are Black, well you won't stand a chance as they will try to everything under the sun to get you into trouble. Avoid them at any cost*"

It is interesting to note their "vision and value" statement: "*Our people are what make LCS the success story that it is. We pride ourselves not only on the individuality of our lawyers and support staff, but also on their ability to abide by a strong team ethic to get the results our clients demand, expect and deserve, and to create an inclusive environment*"

Put slightly differently, "*Our dream is to work together, as a united, cohesive team to make sure that our UREBs rule OK. In this regard, we consider Rupert Eales-White as a HOBP (Hated Offensive Black Person), who is an intellectually inferior being, and should stick to his knitting, the only thing those sorts of people are capable of – boxing, football or athletics, running short distance races only (no stamina for anything more challenging, of course).*

# 7. The after-shock

### ***THE CALM***

I was completely calm, cool and collected well before the end, as I knew what the verdict would be.

I simply walked away and drove home, had a bite of lunch, did a few chores and went to pick my daughter up from the village.

When I told my daughter that I had to pay nearly £1800, as I had been found guilty of travelling more than 50 miles an hour around the round-about and hitting a car on the right-hand side without realising it after my swerve, she was very cross with me indeed.

She had volunteered to be a witness and she would have made a very good one. I had dismissed that, as she was a minor and I was not sure about the position, I did not want to put her to any trouble and I was blinded by my fucking Sword of Truth..

She pointed out that, when we encountered the indentation, we were travelling in a straight line at around 30 miles an hour to take the outside lane of the A243. THERE WAS NO TRAFFIC TO OUR RIGHT, only to our left!!!!

She was very good when I pointed out that I could no longer contribute my half share (£1500) towards the replacement molar she would need implanted after her braces were removed later in the year.

She offered to pay for it from the money she would receive at 18. This made me feel incredibly guilty and I have decided to sell the Nissan. Fortunately, I can take over my wife's car my son has been driving for the last year (he is a struggling actor) and my wife can continue to drive my older daughter's car, which she never uses, as she lives in London.

When my wife got back from her daily climb of Mt Everest, I told her the bad news, describing the gross injustice inflicted upon me. She insisted that that should be the end of the matter, I should pay up forthwith (she, very graciously, volunteered to pay it herself) and suggested that I could have accidentally bumped into the car – basically agreeing with the judge. I calmly agreed that that is what I would do but declined her offer of financial assistance.

After cooking the supper and taking my daughter and Bridey to and from their football practice, I worked to the early hours of the morning, producing the first draft of the previous chapter.

I continued calmly until my son phoned me up in the late morning on the next day – Thursday 22nd April 2010.

## *THE STORM*

So, I enjoyed a prolonged period of surface level calm. I was actually bottling it all up. In the hidden depths, I was wallowing in a sea of suffering – anger at the two little shits who had conspired to produce this travesty of justice and anger at myself at my pathetic performance on the day.

When my poor son phoned from work to talk about some minor matter or other, I burst out in an uncontrollable verbal spasm of pain.

He listened to me and then, when I had finished, said, "*If you feel like that, Dad, then you should appeal*". That suggestion was the most appealing suggestion I had ever heard.

When I told my wife, she hit the roof (she has a very sore head indeed, poor dear). I mollified her by promising to pay the fine and just send the letters to set the record straight.

I have complete sympathy with her, as it has been a nightmare for her as well as me and putting her through the wringer again would have been unforgiveable.

## *THE APPEALING LETTERS*

That evening I composed the following letter and sent it the following morning (Friday) by next day delivery to Miss Black, the Office Manager. She must now be able to recognise my hand-writing and, I would imagine, her heart sinks into her boots, whenever she sees the envelope.

*Dear Miss Black*

*I attended my hearing in front of a Deputy District Judge (whose surname I most unfortunately cannot recall) and was ruled against.*

*I am writing to ask you to pass this letter to Judge Right for her advice as to whether I can appeal. The grounds for such an appeal are the following.*

1. *The claimant's detailed witness statement should not have been allowed to be entered as a valid document, as it was sent within the 14-day period. This was barred by the written instructions contained in Judge Right's ruling of 26th November 2009, which governed the appeal proceedings.*
2. *The claimant's solicitor produced in court a very inaccurate, hand scribbled map of the suggested location of the incident. This should have been debarred according to the same ruling provided by Judge Right. I, stupidly, allowed it, as it enabled me to provide copies of a Google map which demonstrated that my car had not been travelling in either of the two separate locations specified by the claimant. This scribbled representation of the location was grossly inaccurate, which had a material bearing on the decision taken by the judge on location. As this "map" was on a single piece of paper which changed hands, I had no time at all to study it in any detail.*
3. *Throughout the hearing the judge gave 100% accuracy to the claimant's witness statement and completely ignored and discounted my "Statement of Truth". This is despite the fact that my witness statement had been signed by all three parties travelling in the car, and despite the fact that our witness statement was a faithful record of events reported to the police on 27th October 2008, as compared to the claimant's incredibly detailed "Statement of Truth" drawn up nearly one and a half years after the actual incident.*

*4. When I proved that I had not been travelling on the A24, the location specified in the statement's original claim dated 8th April 2009 and when I proved that, if I had been so travelling, according to that statement I could not have been in a collision as all the damage had been on the left hand side and I had "cut across his correctly proceeding vehicle" (from the right hand side), the judge discounted this by pointing out that there were always such inaccuracies in such statements and it was only when you had the witnesses in court that the real truth emerged.*

*I found this statement extraordinarily worrying, as it seems me to completely undermine the fact that "Statements of Truth" should be statements of truth, which is why they are signed to that effect. What was also a little worrying is that the judge treated the claimant's witness statement, written a year later, as the gospel and the written statement a year earlier as being completely inaccurate.*

*5. Finally, I was found guilty of travelling more than 50 miles an hour as I went over an indentation directly onto the A243 to Kingston and when swerving as I went through that indentation, hitting a car on the right-hand side, without noticing either the car or the collision.*

*6. When I mentioned this to my daughter, she was very cross indeed with me as she pointed out that I was only doing around 30 miles an hour. She also pointed out that, at the location of the indentation, we were travelling in the right-hand lane to move directly into the right-hand lane of the A243, and there were no vehicles travelling on our right – just one in front and one behind, neither of which came into contact with our car.*

*I would be most grateful indeed if I could receive an early reply to this letter.*

*Yours sincerely*

*Rupert Eales-White*

When I got home from posting the letter, and had completed a few chores and had my lunch, I had another thought and posted the following letter to Miss Black by next day delivery, which meant she would get them both simultaneously – a double whammy for the most unfortunate lady.

*Dear Miss Black*

*Further to my earlier letter of today, I enclose a Google map of the precise location. I proved in court that I had not been travelling where the defendant claimed that I had collided with his car, but that was not accepted by the deputy district judge.*

*I quote from the claimant's statement, dated the 8th April 2010*
***Para 8***
*I had driven north along the A24 road and had then driven onto the A243. I was driving towards a large roundabout when I intended to take the road for Oxshott and Esher. I was positioned in the right-hand lane of a dual carriageway and I was travelling at about 50 mph. At this point in time I was just passing under what I would call an underpass under another road. I was driving a steady course in my lane.*
***Para 9***
*Quite suddenly I was aware of a black or dark 4X4 vehicle type vehicle that was passing me in the left-hand lane, undertaking me in fact. As it passed, it cut across to its right very close to me and I felt a bump as it did so. I immediately swerved to my right but because of the location I was in, there was a wall to my right along the centre island at this point. I virtually immediately swerved back again to my left.*
***Para 10***
*I realised the vehicle had struck me (and so on).*

*As stated to the police on 27th October 2008, I was travelling from Warlingham to Kingston-upon-Thames via the M25. I joined the M25 at junction 6 and came off the slip road at junction 9. I proceeded round the round-about and took the A243 Kingston Road.*

*Clearly, I never travelled on the A 243 Kingston Bypass, Kingston and clearly, I was not the vehicle involved in the collision with the claimant's vehicle.*

*Could you please pass this letter on ASAP to Judge Right*

*Many thanks etc.*

### ***THE JUDGEMENT***

I had proceeded swiftly in this matter, as I wanted to get my letters in before the judge got around to issuing his judgement, which, if historic precedent was anything to go by, could take a matter of weeks. After all, judge Right did not issue her judgement until 26th November, with the actual ruling taking place on the 5th October.

The deputy judge's UREB had anticipated that I would not take his ridiculous ruling lying down. His judgement thudded through the post on Monday, at the same time as my appealing letters bumped (or should I say "crashed") into Miss Black. It was dated the day after the hearing, i.e. Thursday 22nd April.

UJ3 had advised us that he was terribly rushed, before he spent an hour and a half luxuriating in producing my humiliating defeat, and so he must have put in a little bit of overtime – poor man.

What stresses and strains are imposed on these dedicated men as, driven by their deeply held sense of duty, honour and fair play, they go that extra marathon in their noble service to Her Majesty the Queen.

It was short and sweet (ish).

## ***General Form of Judgement or Order***

*Before* ***DEPUTY DISTICT JUDGE UJ3*** *sitting at Y County Court* (and address)

*Upon hearing Counsel for the Claimant and Defendant in person*
***IT IS ORDERED THAT***
*Judgement for the Claimant in the sum of £1,759.68 payable by 5 May 2010.*
*Dated 21 April 2010*

## *KEY POINTS*

No "forthwith". No warnings and threats and no address as to where to send the money (which I knew had changed from the previous judgement.) - a rush jobbie with 5th May close enough in to make starting an appeal a very remote possibility.

So, I wrote out my cheque and sent my final communication to ARS. I must admit that I took a lot of pleasure in my last communication in this whole disgraceful affair.

*Dear ARS*

*I enclose a cheque for £1,759.68 in settlement of the judgement against me.*

*The Deputy District Judge, showing an unprecedented speed in getting his judgment out (posting the day after the hearing must be an all-time record) failed to advise the address for payment and I know that it has changed from the last judgement against me on 12 August 2009.*

*So, could you please make sure the cheque is delivered into the right hands and send me a receipt. It would be most unfortunate for me if I failed to meet the rather tight deadline of 5th May and you were "forced" to send another of those jolly little letters: "If I do not receive payment, I will take immediate steps to enforce the judgement without telling you in advance (for instance by sending Bailiffs or High Court Enforcement Officers to your house.) You will then have to pay any additional costs our client incurs in enforcing this judgement against you."*

*And I certainly want to avoid my daughter being psychologically traumatised again and hiding her lap-top under the bed, whenever she goes to school.*

*However, in the spirit that has pertained throughout this lengthy matter of open and honest exchange of accurate and truthful information, I am delighted to advise you that I am writing up this case in the necessary detail, with all the players playing their appropriately starring roles, in the form of a book. This sets out exactly why and how this gross miscarriage of justice occurred as well as containing recommendations for effective change.*

*I am even more delighted to advise that the book in draft form has been accepted for publication. I had lined up a publisher and was just waiting for the final curtain to fall – though I did not realise just how fantastically well it would all turn out in the end.*

*You must really get hold of the book, as the chapter about the hearing with the title, "The Stitch Up," will be compulsory reading for any aspiring lawyer, or judge for that matter, and enable them to reach the incredible standards set by the two inspirational role models.*

*I am sure your relevant colleagues, if not your good self, will be truly excited by the list of people who will be simultaneously receiving signed copies of said book.*

- *The Lord Chief Justice*
- *The Master of the Rolls*
- *The Prime Minister*
- *The Minister of Justice*
- *The Attorney General*
- *The Law Officer in the House of Lords*
- *The leaders and justice ministers and law officers of the opposition parties*

*And now I must end. "Parting is such sweet sorrow". Yet needs must be when the muse summons. I have to bid you, ARS, adieu.*

*Yours sincerely*

*R.M.D. Eales-White*

To complete the picture, I received a letter from ARS on 4th May confirming their receipt of my cheque and that they were going to close the file very shortly!

The **male diary manager** (not Miss Black) from the County Court, wrote a letter to me, dated 6th May, and advised me that the district judge had stated that, as judgement had already been given, the "*matter cannot be reconsidered*" and "*if you are unsure of your position you should seek legal advice*".

*Note:*

As you will discover, the date on this letter is critically important. More-over, given the male diary manager and not office manager replied, as previously, there is a clear implication that UJ2 had given instructions to ensure that Miss Black did not get any letters from me or, if she did, they had to passed directly to him.

# 8. My fight for justice

Having received the reply from the male diary manager, I concentrated on completing "The Hidden Truth". Once finished, I sent it to the publisher of the "Succeed" series.

Having appealed to my publisher's highly developed "greed motive", the publisher duly sent an e-mail confirming his acceptance and agreeing the standard miserly terms.

Shortly afterwards, the publisher reneged on his agreement, overcome by a combination of UREBs, gave the standard UREB driven specious reasons, but his prick of conscience (or the conscience of a prick) made him offer to provide me with copies of the book at the very pleasant price of £1.80 a copy, with a minimum order of 50 - the sting in the tail.

So, I ordered 50 copies and sent them out to all the Great and the Good involved in the provision of Justice in the UK. It turned out to be a far longer list than I had advised ARS. I set out below the three relevant documents I sent out to all parties - the list with opening comment, my letter to President Barack Obama via the US Ambassador, and my letter to the Queen.

## 1. LIST OF THE GREAT AND THE GOOD AND THE NOT SO GOOD

I set out below the names, titles and addresses of prominent individuals, to whom I have sent of copy of this book with a call to action to create a justice system that maximises the probability of the discovery of the truth – conscious and hidden - and therefore minimises the incidences of citizens being convicted of crimes they did not commit and the guilty being let off crimes they did commit.

At the end, I attach a copy of my letter to the US Ambassador to London and Her Majesty the Queen.

**Abbot** Diane, Member of Parliament, House of Commons, Westminster, London SW1A 1AA

**Adams**, Gerry, Leader of Sinn Féin, Northern Ireland Assembly, Parliament Buildings, Ballymiscaw, Stormont, Belfast, BT4 3XX

**Alton**, Roger, Editor of the Independent Newspaper, Independent House, 191 Marsh Wall, London E14 9RS
**Amos,** Baroness Valerie, House of Lords, Westminster, London SW1A 0PW
**Arden,** Dame Mary Howarth, Justice of Appeal, Royal Courts of Justice, the Strand, London WC2A 2LL
**Browne,** Desmond, Chairman of the Bar Council, 289-293 High Holborn, London W C1V 7HZ
**Cameron,** David, Prime Minister, No10 Downing Street, London SW1A 2WH
**Chakrabarti**, Shami, Director of Liberty (The National Council for Civil Liberties), 21 Tabard Street, London SE1 4LA
**Clarke**, Kenneth, Lord Chancellor and Minister for Justice, 102 Petty France, London SW1H 9AJ
**Clegg, Nick**, Deputy Prime Minister, 26, Whitehall, London SW1A 2WH
**Cricklaw**, Charles, President of the National Black Police Association, Ground Floor, 24 Laburnum Road, Wakefield, West Yorkshire WF1 3QP
**Dimbleby,** David, Question Time, c/o BBC Television Centre, Wood Lane, London, W12 7RJ
**Dobbs**, Mrs Justice, High Court Judge, High Court in London, Old Pye Street, London SW19.
**Ford**, David, Northern Ireland Justice Minister and Leader of the Alliance Party, Northern Ireland Assembly, Parliament Buildings, Ballymiscaw, Stormont, Belfast, BT4 3XX
**Grieve,** Dominic, Attorney General, 20, Victoria Street, London SW1H ONF
**Hale,** Lady Hale of Richmond, Justice of the Supreme Court, Parliament Square, London SW19 3BD
**Herbert**, Peter, Chair of the Society of Black Lawyers, Tooks Court Chambers, 8 Warner Yard, London EC1R 5EY
**Johnson**, Boris, Mayor of London, 43, Marsham St, London SW1P 3
**Judge**, Lord, the Lord Chief Justice, Royal Courts of Justice, the Strand, London, WC2A 2LL

**Marshall**, Hazel, Judge, Office of the Public Guardian, P.O. Box 15118, Birmingham, B16 6GX

**May,** Theresa, Home Secretary, Home Office, 2 Marsham Street, London SW1P 4 DF

**Nei**l, Andrew, "This Week", 4, Millbank, London, SW1P 3JQ

**Neuberger**, Lord, Master of the Rolls, Royal Courts of Justice, the Strand, London, WC2A 2LL

**Obama**, Barack, President of the USA via the US ambassador to London,

**Orde,** Sir Hugh, President of the Association of Chief Police Officers, 1st Floor, 10 Victoria Street, London SW1H 0NN

**Paterson,** Owen, Secretary of State for Northern Ireland, House of Commons, Westminster, London SW1A 1 AA

**Philips**, Trevor, Chairman, Equality and Human Rights Commission, 3 More London, Riverside, Tolley Street, London, SE1

**Robinson**, Peter, Northern Ireland First Minister and Leader of the DUP, Northern Ireland Assembly, Parliament Buildings, Ballymiscaw, Stormont, Belfast, BT 4 3XX

**Rogerson,** Paul, Chairman SRA (Solicitors Regulation Authority), Ipsley Court, Berrington Close, Redditch, B98 0TD

**Rushbridger,** Alan, Editor of the Guardian Newspaper, Kings Place, 90 York Way, London N1 9GU

**Saunders**. Alan, Head of Crown Prosecution Service in London, Seventh Floor, 50 Ludgate Hill, London EC4M 7EX

**Susman,** Louis B, US Ambassador to the Court of St James, 24, Grosvenor Square, London, W1A 2LQ

**Stephenson**, Sir Paul, Commissioner, Metropolitan Police, New Scotland Yard, Broadway, London SW1H 0BG

**Thompson**, Yvonne, Managing Director, ASAP Communications ltd, 2, Tunstall Road, London SW9 8DA

**Windsor**, Elizabeth, Her Majesty the Queen, Buckingham Palace, London SW1A 1AA

## 2. COPY LETTER TO LOUIS B SUZMAN, AMBASSADOR TO THE COURT OF ST JAMES

**THE HIDDEN TRUTH**

**Ensure our citizens are never convicted of crimes they did not commit.**

Dear Mr Ambassador,

I take great pleasure in giving you a signed copy of the above book. I would also be grateful if you would ensure that the signed copy for President Obama is delivered to him personally. He will be extremely grateful to you as this single act will be of singular service to your country.

You will understand why once you have read the book.

I would draw your attention specifically to THE explanation of the Bradley Effect, as well as why President Obama would not have won the election in 2008, had not the battle between subconsciously held racial prejudice and the self-preservation instinct been decided in his favour.

Racial prejudice is institutionalised both in the UK and the USA because those decision-takers, who are subconsciously racially prejudiced, are not consciously aware of and never consciously admit to the prejudicial acts they commit – necessarily as the prejudice is lodged in the subconscious (the pane of glass in the Johari window which is "known to others" but "unknown to self".)

There is an analogy with Dr Jekyll who was not aware that his hidden Mr Hyde took over his conscious self and committed Hydeous acts on his behalf without his conscious permission.

You will notice that the political decision-takers in the UK to whom I have sent this book are predominately male and white.

Many of them will have had subconsciously held racial prejudice transferred to them by their parents, without any conscious awareness that the transfer has taken place.

This means, when it comes to making the necessary changes detailed in the book to create a justice system that ensures discovery of the truth, conscious and hidden, that the spirit will be most unwilling, as the flesh is white – unless Her Majesty the Queen can, *"gently steer them in the right direction"*.

If you ensure that your President reads the book, you will enable the United States of America to return to the principles of its founding fathers and make them come alive again – ensure that Truth Justice will prevail.

I am delighted to be of service to the USA, as my beloved brother Gavin, who was a dual citizen of the USA and UK, was a victim of 9/11

Yours sincerely

Rupert Eales-White

## 3.COPY LETTER TO HER MAJESTY THE QUEEN

**THE HIDDEN TRUTH**

**Ensure our citizens are never convicted of crimes they did not commit.**

Madam,

I take great pleasure in enclosing a signed copy of the above book.

I do hope that you find the book very insightful and thought-provoking.

If you could gently steer the male of the species in the right direction and lend your invaluable wisdom and experience to enable Truth Justice to prevail in the UK (and not let the US get a march on us!), it would constitute a remarkable legacy on what is already a truly remarkable reign over us.

I have the honour to be, Madam, Your Majesty's humble and obedient servant.

Rupert Eales-White

================

As to response, a minority fell into the black hole. Anodyne acknowledgements or replies from minions formed the majority response. With regard to my letter to the Queen, a Mrs Bonici sent the book back very rapidly indeed, saying that she was not allowed to receive gifts from her subjects. I then wrote to Prince Charles, sending him a copy of the book, the copy I had sent the Queen and asking if he could give it to her.

This was the reply for Mrs Claudia Holloway.

*Dear Mr Eales-White*

*The Prince of Wales has asked me to thank you for your kind letter which came with a copy of your book, "The Hidden Truth".*

*His Royal Highness is most grateful to you for taking the trouble to send him the book. It really was most thoughtful and generous of you, and The Prince of Wales has asked me to send you his warmest thanks and best wishes.*

*As regards the copy of the book that you sent to her Majesty The Queen which was returned with the accompanying letter from Mrs Bonici, I regret that His Royal Highness feels he cannot intervene in or overrule procedures followed by Her Majesty's Household. Should you wish to return this copy, do please let us know.*

*Yours sincerely*

*Mrs. Claudia Holloway*

The only other reply of note was from the then staff officer to Sir Hugh Orde, the President of the Association of Chief Constables in England, Wales and Northern Ireland.

*Dear Mr Eales-White*

*Thank you for sending a copy of your latest book, The Hidden Truth, to Sir Hugh. I will ensure that he receives it.*
*I have briefly perused the contents and I think that it will certainly stimulate some challenging self-reflection amongst those that read it.*

*Yours sincerely*

*Dave Spencer, C. Insp*
*Staff Officer to Sir Hugh Orde OBE QPM.*

A relevant additional point was that some minion wrote a haughty, initialled, rather than signed, dismissive reply on behalf of the Master of the Rolls but did provide his e-mail contact.

And that was the end of that story - zero sales.

In May 2011, the story of Dominique Strauss-Kahn's (former head of the IMF) fall from grace broke. As I believed his actions on the day were driven by his USUs [The UREB "Unfulfilled Sexual Urges"], I wrote another book, "Invisible Mr Hyde", which included this case.

This too was accepted for publication by the FEMALE editor of a small publishing house, having agreed extremely miserly terms. However, a deathly hush prevailed, and I never got a whisper from this editor again, presumably because the male publisher had intervened on his UREBs' behalf.

However, on the 30th May, I e-mailed a copy to the haughty minion, asking him to forward it on to his boss, the Master of the Rolls, and asking what I should do as wanted to launch an official complaint against the three judges for perverting the course of justice and the county court for gross maladministration of the case. I named all the names.

Answer came there none. So I got a printing company to make up 30 copies, given the unit price below that number was prohibitive, and sent the minion a copy, asking him for the information I had requested to be given to me with 15 working days or I would send a copy of the e-mail, letters and book to the Registrar of the Supreme Court, who had provided me with a polite thanks on behalf the Justices, to whom I had sent, individually, details of "Invisible Mr Hyde", (as I also had to all the High Court Judges in the Chancery Division, Queen's Bench Division and Family Division.)

This produced a very rapid response indeed (for a civil servant), advising me to take my case against the judges to the OJC (Office of Judicial Complaints) and go directly to the County Court about maladministration.

He also advised me that **HE HAD NEVER RECEIVED THE E-MAIL.**

My reply was a tad caustic:

Dear Mr Capon,

I take exception to your arrogant squiggle with no name after, masquerading as a proper signature to your letters.

The contents of your letter of 17th June are noted. I would point out that you have proved that you are human, driven by unrecognised biases.

You state that you did not receive my e-mail of 30th May, which is in stark contrast with the e-mail residing in my in-tray from your good self which contained the following information:

*"I am away from the office until the 6th June 2011. I do not have access to my e-mail during this period. If the matter is urgent, I can be contacted on 07931 846468."* (Number Changed)

Yours sincerely, Rupert Eales-White

So, I wrote to the office manager launching a complaint against the court for maladministration and enclosing a copy of my letter of

23 April 2010, which I had written via Miss Black to District Judge Right to appeal against the adverse judgement made against me by the Deputy District Judge two days earlier. I also mentioned that I had launched an official complaint with the OJC against the three judges. (Very, very, very stupid of me in hindsight.)

This letter must have winged its way at the speed of light to UJ2. UJ2 had a dilemma. The male diary manager could hardly reply. The reply had to come from Miss Black.

It duly came with the standard specious reasons as to why there was no case to answer, and no reference to the incriminating evidence. In short, case closed.

What happened with the OJC was truly fascinating.

- I provided the case worker assigned to me with all relevant information and evidence, including all the weighty evidence to support my hypothesis that UJ2 had continued the perversion of justice by his interception tactics.
- The case worker advised me that I could choose between taking my case via their good selves to the Lord Chancellor or the Lord Chief Justice.
- Without a moment's hesitation, I plumped for the Lord Chancellor.
- Subsequently, I was advised that this case worker had been "let go".
- To cut a long story short, I was finally advised by the Head of the OJC, that the matter had been submitted to the Lord Chief Justice, who had ruled it was out of time, as I had failed to appeal against the judgement within a fortnight of it being made.

*Note*

At no stage until the final letter from the Head of the OJC had I been advised of this incredibly short time period - not by Mr Capon and not by the case worker, who would not have accepted the case if it was true (and so had to be sacked). Incidentally, the letter from the diary manager was dated 6th May. This is precisely 15 days after the 21st April.

Of course, on reflection, there would have been an "old boy's network", though the Head of the OJC at the time was female. There was no way that the case could ever see the light of day.

I would imagine that the Head of OJC acted ultra vires.

If it did reach the Lord Chief Justice, which I doubt very much, then there is no way he would ever let it see the light of day.

Our UREBs make liars of us all, which leads neatly to the next chapter covering the two methods to eliminate those nasty little creatures.

*Note:*

We all have blind spots. As I write this note (14th January 2017), I have just discovered one of mine. I have read the above section on the OJC many many times before and have just finished checking for typos. As I did, I realised that all this "failure to appeal against the judgement" was a complete and utter red herring, which I swallowed hook, line, and sinker.

I was not trying to launch a very late appeal against my 21st April 2010 sentence. I was taking a case against the three judges (whose careers and reputation would have been ruined if their actions had been revealed), where, of course, a fortnight's time limit would not apply.

When you receive a letter from the Head of OJC stating that your case has been ruled out of time by the Lord Chief Justice, you believe it automatically. In any case, I had no-where else to go, even if I realised the truth of the matter.

It just goes to prove once again that UREBs are very, very, very devious and dangerous beasts.

# 9. Eradicate unrecognised biases

As mentioned, if we commit a UREB driven act, we are, to use my father's biblical phraseology, SINNING IN IGNORANCE and so can never stop sinning. This has unpleasant outcomes when we shed our mortal coil or go to meet our maker or face the Grim Reaper.

- If we are Protestants, then eternal hell and damnation awaits us.
- If we are Catholics, we might get away with a few millennia in Limbo after wearing out our Rosemary beads.
- If we are agnostics or atheists, we might be put off by the fact that our nearest and dearest, if there are any left, will dance on our graves or scatter our ashes with a hip hip hooray.

One of the abiding lessons I learnt from my brother's sudden tragic death was that, when we hear the sound of the last trumpet, if at all possible, we should be wafted to wherever or nowhere in the warm embrace of love, in the last moments of the present and future and memories of love in the past.

Put simply, do you want to die a reformed Scrooge or Jacob Marley, Scrooge's deceased business partner, now a chained and tormented ghost, damned to wander the earth forevermore as punishment for his greedy, selfish and uncaring attitude towards mankind.?

## METHOD 1.

Now my writing mentor is Bryan Smith, who wrote a commentary for "Succeed at Work" and used to be Director of Studies at Sundridge Park Management Centre and is still, aged 75, editor of "Industrial and Commercial Training" for which I have written numerous articles. He stopped his consultancy work a couple of years ago.

He is an expert on "cultural diversity" and was employed, mainly in the public sector, to run workshops to overcome the serious problems caused in the workplace by sexism, racism and homophobia. He discovered that those people who admitted their prejudices, invariably were those who took positive and effective action to eliminate them, so that they re-create a positive self-image. Those, who would not admit to them, were incapable of any change.

*Note:*

I am adding this on the afternoon of 10th September 2016 (a day before the 15th anniversary of my brother's murder by Osama bin Laden), having watched an early episode of the detective series, "New Tricks". The female boss, a detective superintendent played by Amanda Redman, heads up UCOS (Unsolved Crime and Open Case Squad) consisting of three "grumpy old men", all former police officers. The cockney detective is played by Dennis Waterman.

In the episode, involving the Asian community, the Dennis Waterman character is accused, implicitly, by his boss of being racist. In his reply, having explained why he was brought up to be racist, he vehemently denies he is now racist, concluding with the comment. *"Now that is racist.......and it took me a long time to learn any better......a long time to learn that the only way to stop being one....to deal with it....is to admit it."*

Bryan is a very perceptive individual and pointed out an almost universal truth, in part already covered. Whatever types of people we are, white males of our generation from the dominant culture were brought up to be consciously racist, sexist, and homophobic, or, as my best friend once remarked to me: *'being prejudiced against black people, believing that a woman's place was in the home and disliking homosexuals, as they indulged in unnatural sexual practices, was the order of the day'*. Women were brought up to be racially prejudiced, homophobic and believe that their place was in the home.

At the time, of course, these prejudices and the firm belief by both genders that a woman's place was in the home, were re-enforced in the playground and the whites only schools we attended.

What I realised was that our parents were doing their best for us so that we did not become social outcasts and they tried to be "*the best possible parents they could be.*"

No blame to them, and, critically important, no blame to ourselves. No blame, maximum gain.

Now differences are visible daily – whether skin colour, the physiognomy of different races, gender and sexual orientation. I found that once I had been honest with myself as to my historic prejudices, following the no blame rules, my UREBs had gone and I treated different individuals equally. My relationships and decisions were taken based on the individual rather than the visible difference.

I was helped by the fact that my father and hence my good self practised what he preached in regard to dealing with people. It would be considered a quaint phrase today. *"You should treat a coal-miner exactly the same as you would treat the Queen* (of England"). Once I included those categories whom my UREBs had deemed as not "people", the job was done.

## METHOD 2

This method formed the key component of the first chapter of, *"Winning Ways to Work"* (Legend Business, 2011) with the heading, "Achieve all your goals".

It received the following comment from Miles Templeman, Director General of the Institute of Directors (IOD) (2004-2011). *"The focus on the fundamental aspect of setting clear goals and how to achieve them provides valuable guidance to us all whatever the stage of our careers".*

In 2001, I was reading the second module of the material I was sent, when studying for a diploma in performance coaching. I read a case study, to which I gave the title, 'The remarkable 3%'

**THE REMARKABLE 3%**

A very powerful piece of research was carried out using Yale university graduates. They were surveyed in the 1950s, when at Yale, and again 20 years later. **The research showed that 3% were worth more in terms of wealth than the other 97% put**

**together. This 3% also had better health and enjoyed better relationships with others.**

Only one thing fully explained this remarkable 3%:97% split. It was not parental wealth. It was not degree subjects taken. It was not career selected. It was not ethnicity. It was not gender base. It was not any other of the more obvious factors. What produced this remarkable difference was that the 3% had produced written goals in the 1950s. The 97% had not.

Apart from the above advice that writing down their goals contributed to success, I was provided with no further useful information. I eventually solved the problem by discovering Subconscious Psychological Osmosis (SPO) in September 2008, mentioned previously, and the 4th Law of Iceberg Communication Theory (March 2011).

## SUBCONSCIOUS PSYCHOLOGICAL OSMOSIS [SPO]

(Re-stating what you already know).

A given message, if sufficiently repeated, beats on the subconscious and through the process of **S**ubconscious **P**sychological **O**smosis (SPO) seeps from the subconscious to the conscious self under the conscious radar. The result is that the core meaning of the message becomes a consciously held belief. We never recognise the real source of this new belief, as it is hidden in the self-same subconscious. We believe that "*we make up our own minds*".

This subconsciously-driven decision-making process was discovered as the result of reflecting on the outcome of a programme and how it was achieved.

**THE POWER OF 5**

One of my network of tutors ran a 3-day development programme for a law firm. Part of the feedback and review sheet asked the delegates to anonymously assess the tutor on a scale from 1= Very Poor to 5= Excellent.

From the opening of any programme to the end, the walls were progressively covered by flip-charts summarizing key information points, key learning points and so on.

On this particular programme [and only on this programme as I put a stop to the "experiment" as soon as I discovered it], wherever possible and as prominently as possible, the tutor deployed the number 5 and only the number 5, e.g. 5 ways to persuade a client, 5 key learning points, 5 steps to success in negotiation and so on.

It was the only development programme from a suite of programmes that ran for over 13 years, where there was a clean sweep of 5s for any tutor in my tutorial team.

Senior associate lawyers tend to be a somewhat sceptical and cynical bunch. They work themselves into the ground in the hope that they will make partner. They are terrified that they will not make partner. In the absence of the "experiment", the programme would have been well received, as the tutor was competent and well versed in the firm's culture. Hardly any 5s would have been given.

It was no experiment. The tutor was a tad on the "unprincipled Machiavellian" side of things. He had two aims.

The first was to ensure that he was never "let go". The client, understandably, had a "3 strikes and you're out" policy to ensure a high level of performance was maintained. What this meant is that, if any tutor's average rating by the delegates fell below 3.5 on three consecutive occasions, I had to drop him from my network of consultants, to whom I subcontracted delivery work.

In fact, this tutor had "persuaded" me to recruit his best friend to my network and a few weeks earlier, I had had to let his friend go as he fell below the target on three occasions.

His second aim was to put himself in pole position should "I stumble and fall". I took on my fair share of delivery.

I was able to put an end to the "experiment" as my course administrator was also a competent tutor and played the support role on the programme. She worked with me in my "home office" and advised me of what this tutor had done, which, to use a biblical turn of phrase: *"troubled her greatly"*.

I was able to persuade him never to repeat the "experiment". You see - the business I gave him represented 75% of his total earnings. I threatened to cut it in half.

Those senior associates who attended the unprincipled tutor's programme would have flatly denied that their decision-making process had been affected. If they had been presented with the evidence and the reasons, then, being lawyers, they would have recognised the truth of the matter and changed their minds.

## ICEBERG COMMUNICATION THEORY

Imagine you are an Iceberg, floating in the Arctic Circle. The conscious communication is what takes place above the surface. The subconscious communication takes place below the waterline. So only 10% of our communication is driven by the conscious self. A massive 90% is driven from the subconscious self. When two Icebergs (people) meet, their initial communication is below the surface, i.e. from the subconscious. "**First impressions count**". From this reality are derived the three existing Iceberg laws.

<u>*Note*</u>

A key point I would make is that the percentage figure of 90% is an exaggeration, plucked out of thin air to introduce the seductive metaphor of people as Icebergs. Most of us spend most of the time in the rational adult ego state, behaving as adults – calm, cool and collected – in full control of ourselves and the decisions we take. Some people spend most of their time in a highly irrational, emotional state and the 90% figure would hold true.

## 1. Every stimulus produces a response

Let us take an example. Introverts with a client-facing role can find themselves in what are quite nerve-wracking situations for them. A case in point would be when they are under a three-line whip to attend a networking event with clients or prospects. They have to join a group of stranger TOPs. (TOP stands for **T**he **O**ther **P**erson in the relationship.)

What they fail to appreciate is that one or more members of the group notice them before they speak, either in the act of joining or well before. What they also fail to appreciate is that their body language as they approach, driven by their fears and worries, conveys precisely that the last place they want to be is where they are and the last thing they want to do is what they are about to do.

This stimulus, driven from the subconscious, produces a negative response from the group of – again driven from their subconscious. Their reception meets their worst fears. This compounds the problem for the future. It also drives deeper their feelings of inadequacy and low self-esteem. They then start finding all the excuses they can to avoid such painful events in the future.

This means that they do not meet their business development targets. This is a highly career regressive move. It has a negative impact on their performance, image and relationship with their boss.

Now to the solution, provided to me by an introvert on a development programme, who was the top performer when it came to business development.

First of all, the introvert has to practice at approaching the group in a "cool" way, before attending the event. (How to do this is covered in the final chapter.)

When you, assuming you an introvert, gets there, you look for an odd-numbered group (say, to start with, 3, 5 or 7). Now the nature of group dynamics is that, after introductions and any posturing/superb performances from the practised extroverts, dominating the conversation and so on, the group, whilst physically still together, breaks down into a series of 1-1 conversations. So, there will one individual, who is on their own and isolated. Wait, patience is a virtue, until you espy such an individual. Then, confidently, you go up and introduce yourself to TOP. So, you have joined a group by meeting an individual.

Introverts tend to be good at developing one-on-one relationships. So, they are playing to their natural strengths and staying within their comfort zone. There were two reasons why the introverted guy, who told me this, outperformed all the extroverts.

Extroverts tend to meet many people but not focus on one. By focussing one-on-one, he was able to develop the relationship much further than the extroverts, and almost always arrange for another meeting and get it firmly into diaries.

Initially, the first target TOP could be anyone from the client or prospective client teams. It would be a small client and a junior member of that client or prospect team. As his confidence grew, he would work out who was the big client fish and who was the key player. As soon as that player was on their own or the odd person out in group, he would move in for the profitable kill.

A final point is that, as your confidence grows, and you become more and more successful in the group environment, you become much more prepared to move out of your expanded comfort zone – and join an even-numbered group. Eventually you become not bad at all in group settings and have become comfortable and confident in operating in the *"outer world of people and activity"*.

*Note:*

If you are an introvert, then you will be fascinated in the research findings of the Head of the Training Department of IBM in the UK, provided in 1994. There are three factors which determine your promotion/career success. They are your performance, your image and your exposure - the size of your network to whom you expose your image. The percentage contribution of each factor in large companies was performance a miserable 10%, image 30%, and exposure a whopping 60%. Hence the phrases, *"it is not what you know but who you know"* and *"no network, no job"*.

Clearly, learning how to be comfortable and competent in the extroverted world will do wonders for your career.

## 2. A single detail can produce 100% of a decision

Imagine that you are on the recruitment panel for a company and the panel is faced with two final candidates, who happen to be twins. They are dressed and look identical. They are coming in for the final intensive gruelling. There is a chair placed in front of the interviewers for the interviewee.

The first candidate comes in, and, before sitting down, flicks the cover of the chair and then sits down and says, "Good morning". The second candidate just comes in, sits down and says, "Good morning". Which would you be inclined to choose, assuming you had to make a choice before either candidate had spoken a word?

Everyone goes for the second candidate. However, they reverse their decision if they are told that, in fact, their company is a chair manufacturing one. The candidate's job is to ensure that rigorous quality standards are met. It also changes, if they are advised that they have placed a large drawing pin on the chair beforehand to see how the candidates respond!

## 3. You can consciously affect the subconscious behaviour of others and so change their conscious behaviour as a result

The truth of this law has already been demonstrated by the case study, "The Power of 5".

**THE 4th LAW**

I discovered the 4th law, as the result of reflecting during the period 2008/2009, on the answer to a question I had asked a work colleague - how he had managed to change from being a highly stressed individual to one who was almost stress free?

**ACCEPT WITH A SMILE**

Madhav, a psychologist and fellow trainer, was stressed by any event that was outside his control and affected him negatively (as most of us are), e.g. a pile-up on the M25 meaning that he would be late for work, a boss or client suddenly "changing the goal posts" or the regular criticism he received from his boss.

To eliminate this stress, whenever such an event took place, he said to himself *"accept with a smile"*. It took a lot of effort and repetitions before the internal smile was genuine – rather than a ghastly grimace.

He succeeded, when the internal smile was involuntarily and simultaneously mirrored on his face. It was a very minor smile indeed, a swift wrinkling of the lips that was not noticed by the casual observer.

The first genuine internal smile counted as the first successful behavioural change. After 20 repetitions, it had become a habit. He became a very relaxed, stress free individual - second nature.

As mentioned previously, Research by NLP (the Neuro-Linguistic Programming Society, which should be given its real as the BS or **B**rainwashing **S**ociety) states that if you SUCCESSFULLY repeat a new behaviour at least 20 times, it becomes habitual and implicit beliefs underpinning this habit are developed to drive that habit on. This is why, *"old habits die hard"*, as you need to change beliefs that you are not consciously aware exist or are implicit - a tad difficult to do, unless your read this book.

## 4: You can consciously affect your own subconscious behaviour and so change your conscious behaviour as a result

## THE SOLUTION TO THE PROBLEM

Writing the goals down was key, as this enabled the 3% to have a visual record. They are highly likely to have prominently displayed them at home or in the office. They would have frequently read them out loud or to themselves.

The messages would have truly "sunk in" (to the subconscious). What is more, the 3% would have put some means to achieve the desired end for each goal. There would have been a positive action(s) for each goal.

They would have harnessed the power of my 4th Law. Once repetition of positive action had occurred at least 20 times, their positive behaviours would have become habitual. Positive implicit enabling beliefs, replacing their negative implicit limiting beliefs, would have formed to drive that habit on.

The great power of positive action is that bad habits can be replaced by good habits without the need to consciously recognise the existence of any implicit negative limiting beliefs underpinning those bad habits. Few contemplate so doing to preserve a positive self-image, necessary for confidence, high self-esteem and good performance.

If this becomes an iterative process over time, we become very positive people, *"at ease with ourselves"* and *"comfortable under our own skins."* WE HAVE ELIMINATED OUR UREBs

Whilst the 3% had more wealth, better relationships and were healthier than the 97% through sheer serendipity (becoming positive people unintentionally), you can replicate the result or achieve any goal you care to set yourself in any walk of life you choose with complete conscious intent and control.

## SIGNIFICANTLY INCREASING FOOTBALLERS' STRIKE RATE ON GOAL

Application of the 4th law will enable footballers to significantly increase their strike rate on goal.

Even the most gifted striker (and all the players in a non-striking role), invariably, when taking a pot-shot at goal (given no time to pause and take a conscious decision), cannot help themselves but aim straight at the goal keeper.

This is driven from their subconscious, a mind-set inevitably formed, given that the goal-keeper is a large human object (dominating the goal area), who moves a lot (catching the eyes' attention), whereas the goal-posts are relatively small and don't move at all. In short, it is an instinctive response.

To overcome this instinctive response, the footballer should:

Think of any goal-keeper as a fear-inducing object they want to avoid at all costs - giant rat or spider or shark or other animal/insect/fish they fear.

Write down, prominently display and endlessly repeat out loud and to themselves the mantra: *"I must avoid that giant rat* (or whatever) *of a goal-keeper*".

Then start practicing with a real goal keeper, aiming inside the post furthest away from him or her.

Practise, Practise, Practise.

As we now know, sufficient practice produces habitual behaviour that becomes "second nature". David Beckham no longer has to consciously think before he puts in that inch perfect cross. He does it instinctively.

And any footballer can do likewise. In the future, when taking a pot-shot at goal, he or she will instinctively aim away from the goal-keeper and inside the post furthest away from that "frightful" goal-keeper.

He or she will significantly increase their strike rate on goal and become a star in their footballing firmament.

# 10.Radically reduce the re-offence rate of criminals

We start with the case study my wife came across, when studying for her degree in social sciences, and then look at key points and the strategic implications. The case study incorporates the discoveries I made in the 2008/2009 period, necessarily unknown at the time.

**KEEP NO PRISONERS**

This was a social experiment that took place about three decades ago now. Before the experiment, teenagers who terrorised old people – robbing them, beating them and occasionally raping them – were sent to jail. The re-offence rate was around 90%.

With the experimental group, they were not sent to prison, but they had to attend a "remedial" programme. In the first days and weeks, all they did was to watch videos of actors and actresses playing out the shattered lives of their victims.

*"They broke down and cried"*. Their actions had been driven by their UREBs (no doubt generously donated to them by their lovely caring parents). For the first time, they realised the existence of such horrible creatures and, for the first time in their young lives, they realised consciously that they had committed heinous, unpardonable offences.

For the first time in their young lives, they felt guilty and for the first time in their young lives, *"they broke down and cried"*.

They were then given support and coaching for them to help themselves never to commit such crimes again. They were, of course, strongly motivated not to do so, because they had taken full psychological ownership of their crime and wanted to create a positive self-image through "atonement".

The re-offence rate was 4% - the few who were "evil through and through" and "beyond redemption" – totally brutalised by their upbringing.

***KEY POINTS***

Historic practise, when young offenders commit heinous crimes, is that they are sent to prison. In prison, huge UREB affirmation and mutual admiration societies are formed. Senior UREBs teach the young puppy UREBs all the tricks of the trade. So young "criminals", who have the potential to be decriminalised, become hardened, the re-offence rate stays at a steady 90%, and a vicious circle is created and confirmed for all time.

It was the repetition of the video showing the shattered lives of the tearaway teenagers' victims that, harnessing the power of SPO, brought the message home and the UREBs out of the subconscious closet to wither away and die, except for the 4% that were "beyond redemption" or evil through and through.

There is an increasingly popular policy of ensuring that criminals meet the victims, against whom they have perpetrated their crimes. This is a complete and utter waste of time, in my opinion, as that will not flush out the devious little UREB, which, in many instances, drove the criminal to commit the crime, into the open light of conscious day. It may cause unnecessary psychological damage to the victim.

***STRATEGIC IMPLICATIONS***

Clearly, for young new offenders, successful best practice as set out above should be adopted and there should be no imprisonment.

Those who are convicted of criminal acts in the future, who do not represent a threat to their fellow citizens, should receive a suspended sentence, appropriate fine (in fraud cases) appropriate hours of community service and, crucially, the application of UREB identification and eradication strategies.

For the hardened criminals, currently in jail, and those who must return, having re-offended, as they are a threat to their fellow citizens, my recommendations are:

- The application of UREB identification and eradication strategies.
- The development of a work ethic with every criminal works a 35-day week for "pocket money". Included in the concept of work would be studying to gain relevant qualifications. The 35-hour working week acclimatizes to them to the norm prevailing in society, when they are let out.
- The introduction of **MINIMUM SENTENCES**, eradication of parole, and, after a criminal has served his or her minimum sentence, they are let out when "experts" determine that their UREBs have been eliminated.
- Such experts will need to be trained in how to identify and eliminate UREBs – see final chapter. We will call these experts ELDs or **E**xpert **L**ie **D**etectives.

What the case study demonstrates, of course, is that, if you can create an environment where any offender recognises and consciously acknowledges that these UREBs exist within themselves, then the vast majority no longer consciously sin.

Re-offending becomes a blip on a crime free horizon. The result will be that threats to society are removed, as the criminals, who are evil through and through, never get out to re-offend, those that are let out rarely re-offend (90% to below 10%) and progressively the prison population is decimated. Within, say, five years, we would have the lowest per capita prison population in the civilised world.

# 11. The expert lie detective (ELD)

In this final chapter, we set out all the tools, techniques and skills to become an expert lie detective (ELD). Specifically, we cover:

- "Cool" communication.
- The reflective listening technique to change some-one who is very angry with you for a mistake you have made into some-one who thinks you are the "best thing since sliced bread" – change an angry lion into a docile lamb.
- The "cool" pause.
- Dealing with TOP (**T**he **O**ther **P**erson in the relationship) when in Hyde mode, throwing a temper tantrum, or in Spock mode – cold, distant, logical and critical.
- Asking the right question.
- Active listening.
- Case studies of effective questioning and listening.
- Harnessing the power of empathy.
- Detecting lies by reading body language and deploying the mathematical technique 'reductio ad absurdum". This can be deployed in face-to-face discussions or examining the writing of a complete stranger. It means *"reduction to an absurdity"*. If you can prove that, following the logic of what an individual said or wrote produces an absurdity or completely untenable position, then it means that the opposite of what was said is the truth. Hence the phrases *"no smoke without fire"* and *"methinks he doth protest too much"*.

  In fact, I conclude this book by the application of this methodology to prove that both the then President Bush and Prime Minister Blair knew that Saddam Hussein had no WMD months before the invasion of Iraq. (I submitted the proofs to the Chilcott enquiry.)

**"COOL" COMMUNICATION**

We start by looking at the three factors that contribute to effective communication. These are what we say, how we say it, and our body language. The table below sets out what constitutes each factor and the percentage contribution.

| Factor | Description | Contribution |
|---|---|---|
| ***What we say*** | Actual words used | 7% |
| ***How we say it*** | • Tone of voice – cold through to warm<br>• Inflexion – way the tone changes<br>• Pitch and emphasis<br>• Speech patterns – fast, slow, hesitant<br>• Use of pauses | 38% |
| ***Our body language*** | • Use of the eyes – the window to the soul<br>• Gestures<br>• Body posture | 55% |

With body language at 55%, we can see how important it is to adopt a body language that is appropriate to the situation we face. That is why explorers, seeing tribesmen advancing on them with spears raised, made themselves look smaller, put a broad smile on their faces [instead of the rictus of fear that would naturally appear] and advanced slowly and humbly with both hands palms up to demonstrate the absence of any weapon.

The three main types of behaviour are:

1. Aggressive behaviour.
2. Assertive behaviour to which we will refer to as "cool" behaviour, because the word "assertive" can overemphasise the ego, and grate on the receiver's subconscious – "I, I, I".
3. Passive behaviour.

The table below sets out the 93% for each type of behaviour, separating out into voice, speech, eyes, face, body and feeling.

| | **Passive** | **Cool** | **Agressive** |
|---|---|---|---|
| ***Voice*** | ❑ Sometimes wobbly.<br>❑ Tone may be singsong or whining.<br>❑ Over-soft or over-warm.<br>❑ Quiet, often drops away at the end. | ❑ Steady and firm.<br>❑ Tone is middle range and warm.<br>❑ Sincere and clear<br>❑ Not over-loud or quiet. | ❑ Very firm.<br>❑ Tone is sarcastic, sometimes cold.<br>❑ Hard and sharp.<br>❑ Strident, often shouting, rise at end. |
| ***Speech*** | ❑ Hesitant and filled with pauses.<br>❑ Sometimes jerks from fast to slow.<br>❑ Frequent throat-clearing. | ❑ Fluent, few awkward pauses.<br>❑ Emphasizes key words.<br>❑ Steady, even pace. | ❑ Fluent, few awkward hesitancies.<br>❑ Often abrupt, clipped.<br>❑ Emphasizes blaming words, often fast. |
| ***Eyes*** | ❑ Evasive, looking down. | ❑ Firm but not a "stare" down. | ❑ Tries to stare down and dominate. |
| ***Face*** | ❑ "Ghost" smiles when expressing anger or being criticized.<br>❑ Eyebrows raised in anticipation (e.g. of | ❑ Smiles when pleased, frowns when angry, otherwise open.<br>❑ Features steady, not wobbling.<br>❑ Jaw relaxed, not loose. | ❑ Smile can become awry, scowls when angry.<br>❑ Eyebrows raised in amazement/ disbelief.<br>❑ Jaw set firm, chin thrust forward. |

| | | | |
|---|---|---|---|
| | criticism).<br>❑ Quick changing features. | | |
| ***Body*** | ❑ Hand-wringing.<br>❑ Hunching shoulders.<br>❑ Stepping back.<br>❑ Arms crossed for protection.<br>❑ Covering mouth with hand.<br>❑ Nervous movements which detract (shrugs and shuffles). | ❑ Open hand movements (inviting to speak).<br>❑ "Measured pace" hand movements.<br>❑ Sits upright or relaxed (not slouching or cowering).<br>❑ Stands with head held up. | ❑ Finger pointing.<br>❑ Fist thumping.<br>❑ Sits upright or leans forward.<br>❑ Stands upright "head in air".<br>❑ Strides around (impatiently).<br>❑ Arms crossed (unapproachable). |
| ***Feeling*** | ❑ Guilty | ❑ Confident | ❑ Angry |

As regards the verbal component, the received wisdom is that you combine "I" statements with the "broken record". Looking at each in turn:

**"I" statements.**

When communicating assertively or "coolly", received wisdom is that you use the first person, e.g. "*I need you to get to work on time*", rather than being impersonal, e.g. "*Would you please get to work on time.*" Whilst you should not lay the source of the request elsewhere, "*the boss wants you to get to work on time*", or "*it is company policy that you get to work on time*", or "*according to your job description, you have to get to work on time*", the direct use of "I" can, as mentioned, grate on the recipient's subconscious, especially if repeated. An impersonal statement, therefore, is to be preferred.

**The "broken record"**

The "broken record" means that you simply, in a calm, confident manner, i.e. "coolly", repeat the particular statement [without altering the words used one iota] as many times as it takes, until you get the desired "Yes". You will always be effective, **provided you completely ignore any excuse or reason given for the bad behaviour,** i.e. do not get distracted by, "red herrings".

As we know, the repetition of the same statement operates through TOP's subconscious to produce the conscious agreement: *"Yes, I will get to work on time in future."*

Typically, three times does the trick – the power of 3. Only once, in my personal experience, did it take more – five times to be precise, and that was with an individual, who had completely lost his cool.

If you use "I", although the power of message repetition means that the individual gives away, there is a dislike of the person using the "I" building up in TOP's subconscious, which perceives a desire to dominate and be in control.

So always be impersonal, whether with work colleague, partner, spouse or child. We have the example, where, without changing the actual words used, you repeat the polite request: *"Would you please get to work on time"* or *"Would you please stop hitting your sister"* with a child or whatever.

They key is to develop, through plenty of practice, a range of tones of voice from the "quiet and warm" (almost always to be used in the work-place) to a very firm, cold, consciously controlled, authoritative, raised (but not a shout) tone of voice - very helpful with a recalcitrant child or dog for that matter.

## REFLECTIVE LISTENING

This is an extraordinary powerful and effective technique. Whenever TOP is aggressive towards you for some perceived mistake you have made, use it. It is just as effective, whether the aggression occurs over the phone or face-to-face.

**BETH AND MONTY**

Let us take two people, who are partners – say Beth and Monty. Imagine Monty comes into their living room one evening and shouts at Beth: *"You stupid woman, you promised to do all that photocopying for me by 9. It is now 11, and you have not done it. I have to have it for my early morning meeting. You make me sick, you incompetent fool."*

Now Beth's reply along the lines of: *"How dare you call me incompetent* (selecting the criticism that can be dealt with most effectively)? *Not only have I been busy all day with my consultancy work meeting my own deadlines, I collected the kids, cooked the supper, put them to bed, whilst you sat on your big butt watching the football. Do it yourself, you lazy git"* leads to a total breakdown in the relationship. Monty stomps off to do it himself, shouting and swearing at Beth. Separate beds again for the seventh night in a row.

Well, Monty's communication contained a **fact** that Beth had missed the agreed deadline; a **need** that he had to have the photocopying for his early morning meeting, and an **emotion** – anger towards Beth. All communications have these three ingredients as a maximum.

Beth's reply also had an emotion – anger returned back at Monty; she did not acknowledge the fact that she had broken the deadline, and met his need by telling Monty to do it himself - adding a few insults for good measure.

As mentioned, TOP could be any important relationship - could be your boss, a friend, an internal and external client, or one of your children, rather than your partner. Whenever you have made a mistake (in their eyes) that causes them stress, they will be angry with you and their fact will be your mistake and their need will be for you to rectify it.

Now what is driving their communication? It is their emotion – their anger towards you, driven from the subconscious without conscious awareness and ability to control. Until they have calmed down, it will continue to drive their communication! So, you have to address and only address the emotion first (and sometimes second, third, fourth and so on) until the aggressor has calmed down. Then, and only then, do you address the need. In other words, you have to move them from the emotional controlling parent state to the rational adult state, before you can communicate effectively.

Even when people have recognised the need to address the aggressor's emotional state first, unwittingly they often add fuel to the flames, e.g. *"I can see you are a little upset Monty"*. To which comes the reply. *"I am not a little upset, as you put it, Beth, I am very angry"*. The secret is never to understate the degree of emotion, but deliberately overstate it. *"I can see that you are really furious with me, Monty, and I am sorry to have caused it"* (or words to that effect). *"I am not furious – just a bit annoyed"*, comes the reply.

There is a very subtle psychological process at play. When individuals are in aggressive mode, they simply want you to do what they want straightaway. Mentally, they are itching to have a fight with you, and will be subconsciously driven to disagree with anything you say.

So, when you understate the emotional intensity, they have to disagree and say: *"I am very angry"*. Now, if some-body says out loud that they are very angry, the need for street cred and the power of auto-suggestion mean they must become very angry. As I said, you pour fuel on the flames, and get severely burnt as a result.

The converse, therefore, holds true. They automatically disagree with your statement that they are very furious, and counter with the statement: *"I am, actually, only a little bit annoyed"*. Then they start becoming only a little bit annoyed. This process is helped by the fact that, again subconsciously, they want to avoid the wrong label. Reverting to the work situation, lots of bosses don't mind having a reputation of being a firm, authoritative leader. Few want the label of *"Mr. or Mrs. Furious"* in the company!

So, after a "cool" pause or ten (see next section), Beth calms Monty down by explicitly acknowledging his emotion and exaggerating it. Then Beth (as a superwoman I appreciate!) should continue. *"I will make sure that it is on your desk before I go to bed to-night"*. If Beth had proceeded along these lines, Monty would have apologised profusely, and the double bed would have been fully occupied. (Of course, either the male or the female could be the aggressor – so the roles could be reversed.)

Another enormous benefit of reflective listening is that, at no point, do you either acknowledge or apologise for the "mistake" (only for causing the emotion), and so you do not have to justify it. You leave TOP with the memory of competence rather than incompetence. If you had apologised for the mistake, you have admitted it and aggressive TOPs typically don't like listening to a load of excuses or "whining". If you go the non-reflective listening route, you just confirm your incompetence in their eyes.

Also, critically, there are always two sides to any "mistake". For instance, I may miss a deadline, I promised my boss I would meet. My boss then perceives that I have made a "mistake". However, my boss is endlessly dumping work on me because he is such a can-do creative genius, never provides proper briefing and I am stressed out of my mind trying to meet his ridiculous deadlines (never true deadlines – the work just sits on his desk day after day). So, I am a living saint with a boss from hell. He should be grateful that I am so loyal and competent that I achieve as much as I do.

No, a great idea to use, "reflective listening", to avoid heated discussion of "mistakes". Incidentally, the reason why the technique is called, "reflective listening", is because you *listen* to the emotion and *reflect* (and exaggerate) that back before addressing the need, and ignoring the "fact".

## THE "COOL" PAUSE

You pause for a few moments to "clear your head" of emotions and stay in the adult ego state, avoiding the instant uncontrolled emotional reaction – the stag response provided by Beth or the wimp response: *"Yes, Master. I am a doormat for you to tread on. I will obey instantly, and I will honour you in the process by walking backwards from your Lordship's presence, bowing and scraping as I leave."*

So, you indulge in a little bit of "heavy breathing". Breathe in deeply, hold your breath for a few seconds, exhale fully and hold your outbreath for a few seconds. The aggressor does not notice what you are doing as they are consumed by anger towards you, and it enables them to hear (internally) what they said and how. A little bit of guilt creeps in and they begin to start calming down, having "let off their steam"

When TOP is angry with you, you need to pause for a few moments to "clear your head" of emotions and stay in the adult ego state, avoiding the instant uncontrolled emotional reaction – the stag response provided by Beth or the wimp response.

## ASKING THE RIGHT QUESTION

We start by looking at closed questions.

Closed questions require a "Yes" or No" response. They usually begin with an auxiliary verb, e.g. "Do you? Is it? Shall we? Could you? The four effective uses of closed questions are to:

1. Confirm facts, e.g. does 2 and 2 make 4?
2. Acknowledge an emotion, e.g. are you angry with me?
3. Push for a decision, e.g. will you marry me?
4. Avoid a conversation, e.g. "Did you have a good week-end?" is much better than saying to a colleague on a Monday morning: "How was your week-end?" TOP might just answer you! With the time-saving closed approach, if the answer is "yes", you can reply "great" and move away, having completed the social nicety in record time. If TOP says "no" and it looks as if there is

much more to come, you can hastily intervene with: *"Sorry to hear that; must dash; catch up with you later to get all the gory details,"* and then off you go – again in record time. "Did you have a good week-end?" is much better than saying, "How was your week-end?"

We tend to use closed questions and avoid open questions – especially as we grow older! This tendency can severely limit the quality of our communication and our ability to have constructive discussion. The four primary reasons for this imbalance are:

1. We are educated into logical thought processes and to find answers.
2. Open questions generate uncertainty, as we do not know what the answer will be. This can cause some psychological discomfort especially for controlling types, whose use of closed questions has become habitual in order to get their own way: *"Am I right or am I right*?" *"I have proved my point, have I not*?"

   There can be the perception of loss of control of discussions, if we don't stick to closed questions. (It is only a perception. The reality is that those who ask probing, open questions control the discussion, as all good interviewers (and negotiators) know, as do all those who have been at the receiving end.)
3. Closed questions save time (as in the social example above) and time is very precious to us all.

As mentioned in chapter 6, "The stitch-up", because of logical thinking, though life is grey (a mix of black and white), we are all forced to think in black or white.

Setting out again the examples from that chapter.

*"Guilty or not guilty". ", me Lud, I think I am 23.56% guilty for the following reasons."*

*"Were you standing next to the murder victim, whom we have established you hated, with your hands covered in his blood"? "Well, actually..." "Just answer the question put to you – yes or no." "Yes" –* ***30 years for murder***.

*"Well, actually, I was going to say that when I came around to have it out with him, I found him with his throat cut. Now I did not like him very much, as he had been horrid to me. But I get upset if a*

*little bird dies, never mind a fellow human being. So, I tried to stem the flow of blood. Before he died, he looked at me and asked for forgiveness. Of course, I forgave him. He died with a smile on his face." One more, "**miscarriage of justice**".*

Turning now to open questions, we start with a poem by Rudyard Kipling.

*"I keep six honest serving men*
*They taught me all I knew*
*Their names were What and Why and When*
*And How and Where and Who?"*

You cannot answer an open question with a "Yes" or "No". That is why they "open" up a conversation, rather than closing it down. However, their value varies considerably.

**Where**, **when** and **who** are focused fact-finding questions, i.e. place, time and person. They are not very "open".

**What**, **why** and **how** "promote discovery". They are the core to effective coaching and enable the deepening of any relationship. Be careful when using why personally or critically, as that, can cause offence and rapidly reduce the quality of the relationship. The trick is stay "cool" and always ask the question in a warm tone of voice.

It is also helpful to reduce the bluntness and brevity of "why" by paraphrasing into a longer introduction:

*"It would help me understand the situation better, if you would give me your reasons for doing this?"*

*"That's an interesting suggestion. Tell me why you think it is the best way forward?"*

*"So, please, tell me the assumptions you made, when you did that?".*

## ACTIVE LISTENING

There are eight ways to becoming effective or active listeners. These are to:

1. Be committed.
2. Be objective.
3. Suspend judgement.

4. Check for understanding.
5. Use positive body language.
6. Use words.
7. Ask follow-up questions.
8. Appreciate silence.

**1. BE COMMITTED**

We need to recognise and believe in the power of effective listening – that, unless we listen effectively, we have wasted all those good open questions. We have to want to listen, "actively". "Actively" is an excellent word, because it conveys the reality that we have to consciously act to listen.

**2. BE OBJECTIVE**

We need to think, make that deliberate pause, and take that deep breath. It is our feelings, our opinions, our prejudices (whether against TOP or the content) or our nerves which deny us effective listening.

The effective listener learns how to take control, not of others, but of themselves. Taking the time out, as a discussion starts, to say to ourselves *"I am going to listen"* will improve our skill. Deliberately pausing, when that comment comes which will trigger an instant negative logical or emotional response, will improve our skill. In short, being proactive, not reactive.

Only when we have listened to ourselves can we listen effectively to TOP.

**3. SUSPEND JUDGMENT**

If we judge before TOP speaks, we don't really listen. If we judge in the act of listening, there are two outcomes:

**We disagree**

If we don't want to express our disagreement, we will be turned off and lapse into passive listening, thus denying an effective conversation. This passive listening can lead to the outcome, [which annoys so many TOPs because they don't understand the reason], where we verbally commit to doing things we don't believe in or want to do, and so either do badly or not at all, if we can find a good excuse later!

If we want to express our disagreement, we will move into "listening interruptus", where we do not hear a word TOP says, and are waiting to seize the speaking crown.

The subsequent flow from us of point making and closed questions will deny an effective conversation. This will lead to a quarrel, if TOP responds aggressively to our aggression, the likely response from a controlling type. It will lead to verbal acceptance only, the likely response from a caring type.

### We agree

That may seem fine, but early agreement will lose some little nuances or new angles, because we have stopped listening.

### 4. CHECK FOR UNDERSTANDING

How often do both parties assume understanding, only to be rudely awakened subsequently by actions inconsistent with the understanding assumed? So:

- Pause to recap – summarize the key points TOP has made.
- Get agreement from TOP before moving on – confirm your understanding is complete with an open question.

### 5. USE POSITIVE BODY LANGUAGE

As we already know, the words we speak have only 7% per cent of the total impact in face-to-face communication; the way we speak – the tones, modulation, intensity, phrasing and use of pauses – has 38% per cent of total impact, and our body language – our gestures, posture and facial expression – a highly significant 55 per cent.

If we are listening effectively, then we will display the right body language. If we consciously try to use the right body language, we will probably feel awkward initially, but, with practise, we will become better listeners - develop a natural skill. So, let us consider facial expression, gestures and body posture:

## Facial expression

Facial expressions should reflect the feelings being expressed. If TOP is feeling sad, look sad, if happy, look happy, and if angry, look angry – angry together at the source of TOP's anger.

If you are the source of anger, that's a different kettle of fish. Then, you take a *cool pause* and move into *reflective listening*

If there are no emotions being expressed, as TOP is in logical mode, then look confident and thoughtful. You are in the rational adult ego state or "cool mode" together.

There should be frequent eye contact, but never a glare nor stare. Such eye contact stops you becoming distracted and conveys the message that you are, in fact, all ears.

It is quite helpful to ask for (and invariably be given) permission to take notes. You can then look down to make a note, rather than sideways, over the TOP's shoulder or down to the floor.

## Gestures

Gestures are for the speaking TOP and not the listener. Through using appropriate gestures, the impact of TOP's message is significantly enhanced. Gestures from the listener act as a distraction – a form of non-verbal interruption.

## Posture

There is not a single right posture, as the posture will vary according to the situation – the logic or emotion being expressed, the ebb and flow of the conversation. However, in all situations, a "cool" posture should be adopted, not an aggressive nor submissive one.

For instance, when seated, the listener could take up an open position [neither legs nor arms folded], lean forward slightly, with the head a little to one side, and hands clasped loosely together, resting on the lap.

There are variations such as leaning back slightly to accommodate the other person leaning forward; open posture, with one hand on the chin and the other supporting the elbow or sitting straight with legs slightly apart, each hand resting on the appropriate knee. This last position is the best position for the back and is known as the Pharaoh's posture.

Another technique you can use to help the development of empathy, about both posture and action, is *reflection* or *mirroring.* You will have all experienced this. At one of the many hundreds of course dinners I have hosted, I and three delegates, sitting around the corner of the dining room table, got into a long, thoughtful and enlightening conversation. I noticed, at the time, that we were all leaning forward with our elbows on the table throughout, and whenever one picked up their glass to drink some wine, we all did.

So, observe the body language of the speaking TOP and mirror it. You are operating powerfully on TOP's subconscious. The TOP literally sees, "one of us".

**6. USE WORDS**

An effective listener uses words in the right tone to convey the right meaning. There are two aspects – reflection and interest:

### Reflection

We reflect the end of an interesting sentence, e.g. *"You fell off your bike, did you*?" or, to mix it up, paraphrase and expand, e.g. *"That fall must have been a nasty experience for you."*

### Interest

Show interest by those little verbal noises or even words. The murmur "mmmmhuh" [or variations, which I will not try to spell] or "Well, I never", "You don't say" or simply "I agree". <u>"I agree" is always music to TOP's ears.</u>

**7. ASK FOLLOW-UP OPEN QUESTIONS**

The focus should be the "promoting discovery" what, why or how. For example:

- "So why do you think he was so rude to you?"
- "How on earth did you get out of that predicament?"
- "Good heavens, so what happened next?"

## 8. APPRECIATE SILENCE

We tend to dislike silence, and rush in verbally to fill it. A natural discomfort with silence may often impair our active listening, either because we do not pause to collect our thoughts and give a measured response – ask the right question – or we speak when it would have better from TOP's point of view, if we had remained silent.

We can, by being silent, give TOP time to control emotions or gather thoughts, or simply share together a pleasant mood or ambience. As Mozart said: *"Silence is the profoundest sound in music"*.

*Note*

When you have finished listening, you have two choices:

1. Use the relevant open probing question to enable the speaker to continue speaking and you continue listening.
2. Used closed questions to close off the speaker. You can then stop the conversation or make any points you want to make.

## AN EXAMPLE OF EFFECTIVE QUESTIONING AND LISTENING

We now provide two examples of failure and one of success. The context is a telephone conversation between a mother (M) and her 13-year-old introverted daughter (D)

***Conversation 1 - Wrong***

M: "Did you have a good day at school today, dear?"

D: *"Yup"*

Awkward pause.

M: *"I'll be home by 8 o'clock. See you then. Bye"*

D: *"Bye"*

*"I just don't seem able to talk to Jenny these days"*, the mother said sadly to herself.

Note:

The fatal mistake was starting with a closed question. If the child is not keen to talk, you will get that answer and result.

***Conversation 2 - Wrong***

M: "So how was school?"

D: *"S'all right"*
M: *"Do anything interesting?"*
D: *"Nup"*
Awkward pause.
M: *"I'll be home by 8 o'clock. See you then. Bye"*
D: "Bye"
*"I just don't seem able to talk to Jenny these days"*, the mother said sadly to herself.

Note:

Better. At least the mother started with an open question, but then shot herself in the foot with a closed follow-up.

***Conversation 3 –Right***

M: "So how was school, dear?"

D: "S'all right"

M: "So, what was the most exciting event of the day?"

D: *Pause. "Well, Mum, spotty Johnnie was sent to the headmaster by Miss Brown during our Maths lesson".*

M: *"Oh! I see. So why was that?"*

D: *"Because she saw him hit Adam, and she sent him straight to the headmaster. You know how strict the school is on no hitting by anyone. In fact, we didn't see Johnny again that day. The rumour is that he has been suspended."*

M: *"And do you think that is a fair decision, if the rumour turns out to be to be right?"*

D: *"Oh, no, Mum - completely wrong - but that's teachers for you.*

M: *"So, Miss Brown must have missed something - jumped to the wrong conclusion. What did she miss?"*

D: *"It's like this Mum. Adam is an absolute pain - he's always teasing the girls and being generally horrible. In fact, he had just made my best friend Lucy cry by teasing her about her braces and poking her in the tummy. Johnny told him to stop it or else. But Adam continued, and he got what he deserved. But blind Miss Brown missed all that was going on, only saw Johnny hit Adam - and it was only a gentle slap - Adam played it up for all it was worth. Then Miss Brown without asking for any explanation or finding out any facts sends him off to the headmaster. We all feel very sorry for Johnny."*

M: *"Well, that does seem unfair. What do you think can be done about it?"*

D: *"Dunno".* Pause. *"Well, I suppose that, if a few of us went to see Miss Brown to-morrow and explained what really happened, she might listen and do something. Could do that I suppose. I'll phone Mary, Lucy, and Bob to-night and see what they think. I wouldn't talk to Miss Brown on my own. I'll get onto that straight away after Neighbours.*

*What time are you coming home, Mum*?

M: *"I'll be back by 8 at the latest - so I'll see you then."*

D: *"O.K. Mum. I'll tell you what me mates say about seeing Miss Brown. Bye."*

M: *"Bye ".*

**Note:**

The mother asked the right follow-up question – an open probing question that started, as they say, to "peel the onion". In fact, she only used one closed question to push for an answer: *"And do you think that is a fair decision, if the rumour turns out to be to be right?"* She asked 5 open questions.

I have run development programme for lawyers for nearly 15 years. One of the most valuable sessions for them was called "action learning".

These typically lasted a couple of hours. They were split into groups of four, with rotating roles. In turn, they played the Q&L (questioner and listener), the PH (problem holder) and two observer roles.

Now, most lawyers' quota of questions is dominated by the closed variety. Also, they frequently use critical Why with a harsh, cold tone of voice. Lawyers are frequently in Spock mode, when not in Cool mode.

So, I introduced a key rule. As Q&Ls, they were only allowed to ask open questions, with one observer focussing on whether they were successful or not. There was, of course, a feedback and discussion session after each role-play, so that there could be rapid ascent up the learning curve.

A few, almost always female, were brilliant. Most were not. Almost invariably, they would start with an open question along the lines of: "so how would solve this issue". They then, without pausing for breath, proceeded to provide the PH the answer at some considerably length.

It was a painful but very effective "voyage of discovery" – discovering the power of what I call the "discovery kings" (what, why, and how) that promote discovery in TOP. Invariably those lawyers who only used open questions *"delighted their clients"*, as the problem-holders had discovered for themselves the solutions to what had appeared intractable work or non-work-related problems. They were very pleased with themselves and pleased with their colleague who had help them to produce this outcome.

Now practise produces proficiency. So, the more you practice, the more proficient you will become. Eventually, you will be beloved by family member, friend, work-colleague and internal or external client alike.

## HARNESSING THE POWER OF EMPATHY

In the example provided, empathetic effective questioning and listening significantly improved the quality of relationship between mother and daughter as the mother managed get on to her daughter's wavelength – tune in.

Where the objective is different e.g. to determine whether TOP should be recruited or promoted or has committed a crime, empathetic questioning and listening (always talking in a warm tone of voice and never challenging or questioning or commenting on what is said but gently lulling TOP into a false sense of security) is extraordinarily powerful in getting TOP to reveal what they intended to conceal, with them being completely unaware that they have just shot themselves in both feet.

In 2006, a colleague and fellow author John Van Maurik were put in charge of the recruitment of 6 new consultants to join the PA Development Practice.

[In 2004, the CEO had exhausted all the profits of Sundridge Park Management Centre as the result of a very badly timed (middle of 1990-1992 recession) vastly expensive expansion into the far east. I thoroughly enjoyed it, as I had 7 memorable trips to Malaysia, running three Developing Human Resource Strategy programmes with another colleague Grahame Morphey and four Strategic Leadership for Results programmes with John Van Maurik. The trust had been broken and we had been integrated into PA Consulting Group, which was a harsh command and control culture where we became electronically controlled – but that is another story. In fact, I studied the year end 2007 accounts, and realised that the PA's Chief Executive, who was a bit of a command and control freak, had bought Sundridge Park Management Centre simply to do a bit of asset stripping when the time was right. He had put a vastly inflated value on the property and was charging us a rent that took up over a third of our turnover.

Fortunately, in March 2008, I was spending a fortnight in Hong Kong, running 5 two-day team-building programmes for the associate lawyers of their Hong Kong office. Now, fortuitously, their

Personal Director, Martin Pexton, was visiting their far eastern offices – Bankok, Singapore, Hong Kong and Shanghai and we met up and had a very boozy meal in one of the top restaurants in Hong Kong. It was during the course of that meal that he made me the offer I could not refuse – guaranteeing 40 days' work at the equivalent of my annual salary. In return, I reduced my daily rate from £1750 to £1400. So, I put in my 6 months' notice and at the end of October 1998, I set up DTS Ltd – incorporating at Martin's advice – to avoid litigation by PA for stealing their clients. I stole all the other clients I had at the time.

In 2000, the assets were stripped, and the majority of consultants were made redundant, including John Van Maurik.

There were 3 stalwarts, who accepted job offers from PA and all took early retirement within 2 years. The three other consultants who went on to have successful careers were 3 of the 6 we recruited in 2006. I would imagine that the New Head of Practice (a successful academic rather than businessman and a truly delightful individual) initiated the expansion to overcome the terrible burden of the rental charge. I do know, from hearsay, that he had a nervous breakdown and returned to his native Australia, where he had been a professor at one of their universities.

To conclude this note, every year, sometimes twice a year, starting in 2001, a group of us, called the "The Spirits of Sundridge Park" meet up in London to chew the cud and have a pleasant meal]

Revenons a nos moutons. We put the adverts in the appropriate places and, by the deadline, we had 323 applications. We had already produced a template to separate the wheat from the chaff, as well as personalised positive rejection letters.

Within 48 hours, the 293 rejection letters had winged their way to the chaff and 30 invitations for an interview to the wheat. We formed a team of 6 expert interviewers and so we each had five. I can only remember one.

The candidate was female, in her early 40s and I did the usual empathetic questioning and listening. During the course of the interview, it became apparent that she was eminently suitable to get one of the positions. Then she made her fatal error without ever realising it. She became more and more relaxed and more and more expansive as time went by.

I still recall her body posture when she made her comment. We were in comfy chairs around the mandatory table. As she talked, she eased back in her chair and took up a position often adopted by controlling men when in relaxed boss mode - slumped back with their arms crossed around their heads.

She mentioned, as she was now in ego UREB mode and wanted to demonstrate just how successful she was, that she was independently wealthy. I made no comment, of course. The interview proceeded to its conclusion. We shook hands, went our separate ways and a few days later, she received the near miss rejection letter.

We wanted consultants who were going to drive themselves hard in a very competitive world, where the rewards for success were very significant but so too was the cost of failure to meet demanding targets – the sack.

The carrot was there, but so too was the stick. For someone who was independently wealthy, both were useless.

Another example, drawn from "Succeed at Work" is where you can interview a complete stranger and discover exactly what type of person they are – whether extrovert or introvert, controlling or caring, practical or creative, organised or flexible - without them being aware. You can make your decision accordingly.

Linda is interviewing a Guy called Charles for Head of Sales.

**CASE STUDY OF ASSESSING SKILLS**

**Linda:** "Well, Charles, as Head of Sales you will need to make some tough decisions under stressful conditions. For instance, you may need to change the sales mix and focus, gear up very quickly to push a new product line, or, if one product fails or becomes a "dog", pull out quickly and perhaps lay off sales staff. It is always tough at the top. So, tell me Charles, when did you last face what, looking back, was a tough decision in stressful conditions?

Charles: "Funny you should ask that one, Linda. Only six months ago, I had to take one of the decisions you have already mentioned. One of our many product lines began to falter and then sales dropped like the proverbial stone, before settling down at less than half the initial sales volumes. This meant we had to cut costs and where else but staff, the biggest cost of all?

(Linda paused and looked interested but was not distracted by answering this question.)

**Charles:** "So I had to let go half the sale force in pretty short order."

**Linda:** "When you say you had to let go, was it your decision alone?"

**Charles:** "Oh! Yes. Senior managers like me are expected to take tough decision and not involve the Board. I did get the nod from my boss, as a matter of courtesy."

**Linda:** "I see. And how did you set about implementing the decision?"

**Charles:** "Oh! That was fairly easy. There were only 16 sales staff involved and three managers – 19 in all. We aimed for a total of nine and used the opportunity to restructure so there was only one manager who had 8 direct reports. I knew them pretty well, had all their performance target and results, and with Personnel providing additional data from staff reports, it was easy to identify who should go and who should stay."

**Linda:** "So who communicated the decisions to those staff, who were going?"

**Charles:** "Well, I know of senior managers, who pass the buck to Personnel. Not me, I know my responsibilities. I told them the bad news."

**Linda:** "And how did you communicate the news to them?"

**Charles:** "Having agreed the list and the terms we would provide, it was simply a matter of a day of painful interviews with the 10 we were letting go. I saw each individual for about half an hour – gave it to them straight from the shoulder, no other way really, explained when they would actually leave, what the financial terms were and gave them a name in Personnel for further counselling and support. (Jane raised an internal smile only at the use of the word "further".)

**Linda:** "And how was morale in the sales force that remained?"

**Charles:** "Took a bit of a knock for a few months afterwards – inevitable I suppose, but then picked up slowly and we recovered to around the same sales to staff ratio that we were at before the whole incident."

***KEY POINT***

When Linda looks at her notes afterwards and reflects on the answers provided, she will find that she has all the information she needs to make a judgement. Charles has demonstrated that he is a competent Extrovert, Practical, Controlling Organiser. Linda will know whether that fits the culture and/or is required for the job.

================

We now turn to the situation where the interview is under considerable stress, which can be at a job interview, performance review session, disciplinary hearing, dealing with a complaint that a key client has made to your boss and certainly if you are being interviewed by the police as a suspect in a crime. TOP is under some form of investigation and knows it. You use this to your considerable advantage.

You start off and continue with your subtle empathetic questioning and listening. Then TOPs makes a little slip of the tongue. It is prefaced by a lowering of the tone of voice and frequently the word "actually". *"Well, actually, I had a little bit of a problem with the client*" (victim). You then pounce and still empathetically say something along the lines of. "So, what was this little problem?". You then pause and wait for the answer. What you don't do, as I have seen so many times take place, is answer your own question. "Where you rude to the client, did he complain about your service, were you late for a vital meeting and so on". You let TOP completely off the hook. TOP seizes upon the answer which has the least downside and agrees with you that that was the problem.

No. You use silence, not to create an ambience, but as a powerful and effective truth tool. You deploy a pregnant pause – as it will give birth to a wriggling little UREB. What happens is that TOP becomes increasingly uncomfortable with the silence. The longer it lasts, the more uncomfortable TOP becomes. Eventually TOP's answer is driven from the subconscious and he says, for instance: *"We had a blazing row as he really gets up my nose".*

The stronger the implicit beliefs, the more powerful the UREB or beast within and the greater the offence.

They will be honest to their true but hitherto hidden natures. So, a giant ego UREB will explain the death of a complete stranger in an act of road rage as the need to avenge the gross insult to its divine status – cutting him up.

The racist UREB will say words like: "I hated the black bastard". The sexist UREB will say: "She was asking for it."

Now UREBs don't always act in isolation. Sometimes situations arise where a set of UREBs combine to produce acts of gross violence.

The headline on page 7 of the Time's newspaper, Tuesday 17th May 2011, was: **FRENCH WRITER COULD PRESS CHAGES AGAINST 'RUTTING CHIMPANZEE'**. The 'Rutting Chimpanzee' referred to was Dominique Strauss-Khan, Head of the International Monetary Fund (IMF), who had been committed to the notoriously violent Riker's Island jail on New York's east river - to await a hearing before a grand jury on the Friday.

First of all, Strauss-Kahn had the reputation of being what is euphemistically termed, "a lady's man". When appointed to the august position of Head of IMF, he would not have been able to give reign to his sexual appetite. He would have been full of USUs – unfulfilled sexual urges. As he would have a very large ego UREB. In addition to being a male chauvinist pig, he would have also been implicitly racist. His USUs and large racist, sexist and ego UREBs combined so that he committed horrendous acts "in the heat of the moment".

According to the Newspaper reports, he had left his room in a hurry and rushed out of his hotel, forgetting his mobile. When he remembered, he rushed back to his room where a hotel chambermaid was making the bed. Her name was Mafissatou Diallo.

According to the charge sheet, the defendant committed the following offences:

- Criminal Sexual Act of the First Degree (2 counts)
- Attempted Rape (1 count)
- Sexual Abuse of the First Degree (1 count)
- Unlawful imprisonment in the Second Degree(1count)
- Sexual Abuse in the Third Degree (1 count)
- Forcible Touching (1count)

When he came to his (rational) senses, he fled the scene of his crime, forgetting to pick up the mobile he had returned to collect.

The charges were dismissed at the request of the prosecution which pointed out serious doubts on Diallo's credibility and inconclusive physical evidence - surprise, surprise. There was, however, an out-of-court settlement, reportedly to the tune of $1.5 million.

To conclude this section, I would emphasis again that you have to exercise a considerable amount of discipline when the pause starts. You become uncomfortable with the pause and have to wait and wait for as long as it takes, otherwise you destroy the object of the exercise - revealing a UREB.

## DETECT LIES

There are 2 ways of detecting lies:

1. Read TOP's body language

2. Use the "Reduction ad absurdum" technique.

## Read TOP's body language

You can always tell if TOP is lying, as TOP cannot control his or her reaction, which is driven from the subconscious.

When we are young children, our subconscious tries to create a pre-lie situation, as soon as we are caught out. So, we put our hands to our mouths to shove the lie back from whence it came. This is unsuccessful.

As we grow older, we become more skilled in controlling this "tell". As adults, we limit our tells to a small cluster of involuntary movements, i.e. looking down to avoid eye contact as well as brushing the top of our lips with a forefinger.

People who need to be skilled liars, e.g. politicians and poker players, train themselves to eradicate these tells. They can look you directly in the eye, and then lie. What most of them don't know is that, **if challenged**, the eyes still reveal the lie. Involuntarily, there is a slight contraction of the pupil - the sophisticated equivalent of shoving the lie back down your throat. Hence the wearing of shades in poker to avoid one expert being able to "read" another expert's bluff.

## Reductio ad absurdum

Once you have learnt to how to ask open probing questions in a warm, empathetic tone of voice, listen effectively to the answer and then ask the appropriate follow up question, you can deploy this technique to uncover the little [ or very large] porkies TOP is telling you. Apart from being very useful with all close TOPs, it is a powerful weapon to be deployed by those who carry out formal interviews - very helpful for recruitment consultants, HR specialists, counsellors, social workers, police officers and lawyers - to name but a few.

It is also, of course, very helpful in the one-to-one coaching role.

Additionally, you never have to meet the "liar" as you can prove from the written word that "people in very high places" are lying through their back teeth, as I have done.

The first two case studies prove that the former President Bush knew that Saddam Hussein had no WMD [Weapons of Mass Destruction], well before the invasion of Iraq, with the scene set in "Saddam Hussein's' catch 22" and "Methinks he doth protest too much" providing the proof.

The next case study, "Who will rid me of the turbulent priest", uses the technique to prove that Dr Kelly's death was not an accident.

**SADDAM HUSSEIN'S CATCH 22**

Bush's sole motive can be perceived as admirable, if not a tad unfortunate. As a dutiful and loving son, Bush was on revenge mission against Saddam to clear the stain on his father's name, caused by the United Nations stopping said father completing the job he had set out to do - topple the hated Dictator.

This is why Bush despised the United Nations and only went through the motions to please his friend Tony.

This is why Bush fabricated evidence to connect Osama Bin Laden to Saddam Hussein, when they were sworn enemies.

We now know that Saddam had no weapons of mass destruction. Saddam knew at the time that he had no weapons of mass destruction. So why did he not throw open his doors to Hans Blix and his inspectors and prove that he had no weapons of mass destruction, thus avoiding a war?"

What I think happened was an extremely Machiavellian trap was set for Saddam, ensuring he was in a catch 22 situation. This strategy was not derived by George, who did not have the intelligence – but by the right-wing mafia. Now the US has such sophisticated aerial reconnaissance that it could spot a soldier smoking a cigarette outside one of Saddam's palaces. Blix's blundering land-based efforts were pathetic – could not have added anything to the search for WMD. They were necessary, as we shall see, but completely irrelevant to the search for WMD.

My answer is that the Americans knew that Saddam had no WMD many months, if not a few years, before the UN inspectors blundered in. Why did they know? Because they had sent Saddam a message that if he did not dismantle his WMD, they would assassinate him. Now Dictators are extremely fond of life, as they have absolute power, have already achieved close to immortality on earth, and are cowards – after all the great Dictator was found cowering in his bearded state in an underground bunker.

So, Saddam dismantled his WMD. With the sophisticated aerial reconnaissance, the US would have watched every move and known when he had completed his task. The mission for the UN inspectors, whether they knew it or not, was not to prove the presence of WMD, but not to be able to prove conclusively its absence.

Once you have a collective conscious mind-set, that would be sufficient to maintain it. Only clear incontrovertible evidence could have altered it. Saddam would have been under instruction to make it impossible for clear proof to be provided in the time available.

Now for the catch 22 for Saddam. His power over Iraq and his position as a dominant influencer in the Middle East rested on his possession and demonstration of WMD, e.g. chemical weapons used on the Kurds and the Iranians – not on the US invaders, of course, as he did not have any by then – no wonder the US knew it would be an easy victory. So, Saddam knew he had no WMD, he knew the US knew he had no WMD, but he also knew he could never acknowledge the truth to the outside world.

Another key point is that many commentators have expressed surprise at the singular absence of planning for the reconstruction after victory. It was absolutely inevitable there was no planning for managing the peace as that was not part of the strategic driver. Bush may have made a few speeches along the lines: "*Give democracy to the peoples of Iraq*", but he was focussed on his vendetta. Remember the incredible resources devoted to catching Saddam, which took many months.

George Bush must have wept with tears of delight at the news of Saddam's capture and cried out loud to the heavens: *"Mission accomplished. Honour restored."* Of course, the death sentence for Saddam was non-negotiable.

Democracy was a convenient cover for a son to avenge his father. It was a great pity indeed that George Bush ever became President of the most powerful "democracy?" in the world.

## "METHINKS HE DOTH PROTEST TOO MUCH"

On the 10th November 2010, on the front page of the Times Newspaper, the attention-grabbing headline was: "WATERBOARDING SAVED LONDON FROM ATTACKS" with the subsequent text all about key extracts from the "world exclusive" memoirs of President George W. Bush.

In the meat on the front page, there was a quote from ex-President Bush from these memoirs, where he shot himself once again in both feet.

The preamble to the quote was that amongst his regrets was the flying of a "Mission Accomplished" banner on the USS Abraham Lincoln [who would have turned in his grave at the actions Mr Bush took], the premature reduction of US numbers in Iraq after the invasion [which took place after his real mission had been accomplished – the capture of Saddam Hussein] and, above all, the inaccurate information on WMD.

Now to the immortal quote: *"The reality was that I had sent troops into combat based in large part on intelligence that proved false"*, he writes. *"No one was more shocked and angry than I was when we didn't find the weapons. I had a sickening feeling every time I thought about it. I still do."*

The Times added at the end of the quote that Mr Bush doubted that WMD might still be hidden in Iraq. I wonder why, Mr Bush?

People who are "protesting too much" do really get their logical knickers in a twist. So, let us assume that George Bush was telling the truth. He expected to uncover large stashes of WMD.

Well, if that was the case, then Saddam Hussein could have used these large starches to give the Coalition forces a bloody nose – with enormous damages to those forces. Indeed, if the stashes were large enough [especially those of chemical weapons], ultimate victory could have been put in doubt.

So, George Bush is saying that he gets a sickening feeling every time he thinks about it - that vast numbers of his troops were not killed or maimed for life and Saddam Hussein might not have been defeated?

**"WHO WILL RID ME OF THIS TURBULENT PRIEST?"**

Now Tony, it has been suggested, was in on the decision to overthrow Saddam very early on in the piece – not that long after Bush's vendetta to topple Saddam became a reality, thanks to 9/11.

As we know, he had an electorate that was very sceptical unlike the US. He never got the same mass support that Bush enjoyed in the US. Hence the importance attached to the United Nations resolutions and hence, when the second resolution failed, the legal advice, deployed in a very clandestine way, that the war was legalised by the first resolution and the second was not required.

This seems to me to be pure chicanery. If that was a fact, then why was there a second resolution?

For Tony, the need to prove that WMD existed was vital to making his case. Hence the dodgy dossier, the 45 minutes to nuclear wipe-out, and the death of Dr Kelly.

My hypothesis is that Hans Blix and his inspectors either knew there were no WMD or were getting mightily suspicious. Now Dr Kelly had been publicly humiliated, and no doubt privately blackmailed to keep his mouth shut. He was extremely bitter at his treatment as a brilliant scientist with inferior terms and conditions to the political jobs worthies. He was on verge of spilling the beans when he was "eliminated".

All the evidence made available suggests that suicide is extremely unlikely, if not impossible. It is also interesting to note how Tony has publicly stated that his greatest regret was the "suicide" of Dr Kelly. Of course, Tony Blair did not authorise the "elimination".

Once a mind-set is established from the top, then there will be always be over zealous, "loyal" servants who will act in the best interests of the Boss, without seeking permission.

The four knights who rushed to murder Thomas à Beckett in Canterbury Cathedral were not under explicit instructions from Henry II. They did receive a helpful hint as to their master's wishes with his question: *"Will somebody rid me of this turbulent priest?"*

If Tony was not racked with guilt at Dr Kelly's murder, and Dr Kelly, a minor civil servant, had actually committed suicide, then why is his greatest regret not the loss of life of his brave British soldiers, or the greater loss of life of the brave US comrades in arms or the even greater loss of life of thousands and thousands of innocent Iraqi citizens?

**THE END**

Printed in Great Britain
by Amazon